DERBYSHIRE FC

BY

JOHN N. MERRILL

Maps and photographs by John N. Merrill.

a J.N.M. PUBLICATION

1988

a J.N.M. PUBLICATION

JNM PUBLICATIONS,
WINSTER,
MATLOCK,
DERBYSHIRE.
DE4 2DQ

Conceived, edited, typeset, designed, marketed and distributed by John N. Merrill.

© Text — John N. Merrill 1988

© Maps and photographs — John N. Merrill 1988

First Published — March 1988

ISBN 0 907496 31 8

Meticulous research has been undertaken to ensure that this publication is highly accurate at the time of going to press. The publishers, however, cannot be held responsible for alterations, errors or omissions, but they would welcome notification of such for future editions.

Set in Rockwell, light, medium and bold.

Printed by: John Price Litho, Brook Street, Bilston, West Midlands.

ABOUT JOHN N. MERRILL

John combines the characteristics and strength of a mountain climber with the stamina and athletic capabilities of a marathon runner. In this respect he is unique and has to his credit a whole string of remarkable long walks. He is without question the world's leading marathon walker.

Over the last ten years he has walked more than 60,000 miles and successfully completed ten walks of at least 1,000 miles or more.

His six major walks in Great Britain are -
Hebridean Journey .... 1,003 miles
Northern Isles Journey .... 913 miles
Irish Island Journey .... 1,578 miles
Parkland Journey .... 2,043 miles
Lands End to John o'Groats .... 1,608 miles
and in 1978 he became the first person (permanent Guinness Book of Records entry) to walk the entire coastline of Britain — 6,824 miles in ten months.

In Europe he has walked across Austria — 712 miles — hiked the Tour of Mont Blanc, completed High Level Routes in the Dolomites, and the GR20 route across Corsica in training! In 1982 he walked across Europe — 2,806 miles in 107 days — crossing seven countries, the Swiss and French Alps and the complete Pyrennean chain — the hardest and longest mountain walk in Europe, with more than 600,000 feet of ascent!

In America he used the world's longest footpath — The Appalachian Trail — 2,200 miles — as a training walk. He has walked from Mexico to Canada via the Pacific Crest Trail in record time — 118 days for 2,700 miles.

During the summer of 1984, John set off from Virginia Beach on the Atlantic coast, and walked 4,226 miles without a rest day, across the width of America to Santa Cruz and San Francisco on the Pacific Ocean. His walk is unquestionably his greatest achievement, being, in modern history, the longest, hardest crossing of the USA in the shortest time — under six months (178 days). The direct distance is 2,800 miles.

Between major walks John is out training in his own area — the Peak District National Park. As well as walking in other parts of Britain and Europe he has been trekking in the Himalayas five times. He has created more than ten challenge walks which have been used to raise more than £250,000 for charity. From his own walks he raised over £80,000. He is author of more than ninety books, most of which he publishes himself. His book sales are in excess of 2 million.

CONTENTS

i

EASTERN DERBYSHIRE

DERBY AND SOUTH DERBYSHIRE

SUPERSTITIONS AND SAYINGS OF DERBYSHIRE

INTRODUCTION

I doubt if any other county of Britain can match the diversity of Derbyshire. It is so rich in every facet — architecture, scenery, industrial archaeology, to name a few. The county's folklore is equally diversified. As I researched and became involved with this book, I never realised just how much material existed. In the end I researched for four years — in local libraries and on the ground — and learnt about more than 250 stories and sayings.

I do not pretend for one moment that it is a fully comprehensive book on Derbyshire Folklore, although I would claim that it is the most comprehensive ever published. Sometimes there is more than one version of a legend, and I have given the one I have found. I know there are others. Even as I write this I have learned of a fifth legend as to how the Chesterfield church spire became crooked. Simply, it was the Devil who, while flying over Chesterfield, decided to rest. He descended to the spire, clung to its side and wrapped his tail around it. When he continued his journey, he left in such a hurry that his tail became caught, bending the spire! As you can see, the process of discovery continues even though I have 'closed' this book.

I have tried to gather my material to give an even coverage of the whole of the county. To many Derbyshire simply means the Peak District, but the Peak District only occupies one third of the county's area. You will still find that the largest group of legends relates to the romantic landscape of the Peak District, but there are also some interesting sections on eastern and southern Derbyshire.

The task of gathering the material has been absorbing and most satisfying. My thanks go to the Local History Departments of Sheffield, Chesterfield and Derby Libraries for their help in finding the information sources — more than 400 — that I needed to gather the material. I am sorry to see it completed, and I can only hope that you derive as much pleasure as I have when you learn the story of a Derbyshire place name, character or superstition.

John N. Merrill.

JOHN N. MERRILL.
WINSTER, DERBYSHIRE. NOVEMBER 1987.

1

THE PEAK DISTRICT

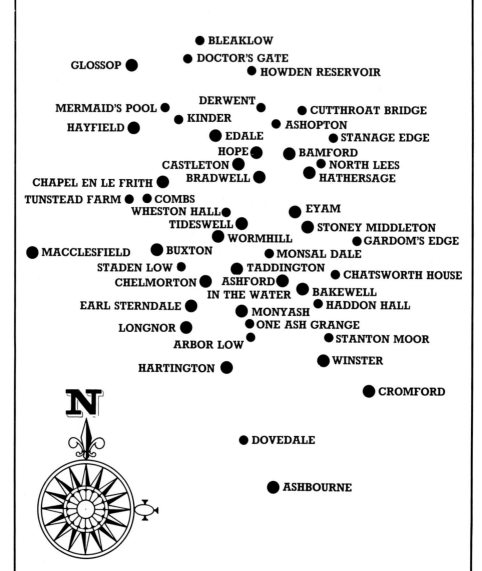

● BLEAKLOW
● DOCTOR'S GATE
GLOSSOP ●
● HOWDEN RESERVOIR

DERWENT
MERMAID'S POOL ● ●
● KINDER
HAYFIELD ●
● CUTTHROAT BRIDGE
● ASHOPTON
● EDALE
● STANAGE EDGE
HOPE●
● BAMFORD
CASTLETON ●
● NORTH LEES
CHAPEL EN LE FRITH ●
BRADWELL ●
● HATHERSAGE
TUNSTEAD FARM ● ● COMBS
WHESTON HALL●
● EYAM
TIDESWELL ●
● STONEY MIDDLETON
● WORMHILL
● GARDOM'S EDGE
● MACCLESFIELD
● BUXTON
● MONSAL DALE
STADEN LOW ●
● TADDINGTON
● CHATSWORTH HOUSE
CHELMORTON ●
ASHFORD ●
● BAKEWELL
IN THE WATER
● HADDON HALL
EARL STERNDALE ●
● MONYASH
LONGNOR ●
● ONE ASH GRANGE
ARBOR LOW ●
● STANTON MOOR
HARTINGTON ●
● WINSTER

● CROMFORD

N

● DOVEDALE

● ASHBOURNE

THE PEAK DISTRICT

IN PRAISE OF DERBYSHIRE

O give me the land where the wild thyme grows,
The heathery dales among;
Where sol's own flow'r with crimson eye
Creeps the sun-burned banks along!
Where the beetling Tor hangs over the dell,
While its pinnacles pierce the sky,
And its foot is laved by the waters pure,
Of the lively murmuring Wye;
O give me the land where the crimson heather,
The thyme and the bilberry grow together.

Arthur Jewitt

THE SEVEN WONDERS OF THE PEAK

During the last three centuries, travellers to Derbyshire visited what were termed the Seven Wonders of the Peak. These were Poole's Cavern, Buxton; St. Anne's Well, Buxton; Ebbing and Flowing Well at Tideswell; Eldon Hole near Peak Forest; Mam Tor above Castleton; Peak Cavern in Castleton; and the seventh — Chatsworth House. There is another ebbing and flowing well at Barmoor, approximately four miles north east of Buxton, but the Tideswell one appears to be the original. Charles Cotton, the friend and companion to Izaak Walton, the fisherman, was a poet who wrote a very long poem about the Seven Wonders, which was published in 1681. The following extracts are taken from this book:

"North east from their fair rivers-head, there lyes
A country that abounds with rarities,
They call them Wonders there, and be they so;
But the whole Country sure a wonder too,
And mother of the rest, which Seven are
And one of them so singularly rare,
As does indeed amount to Miracle,
And all the Kingdom boasts so far excel.
It ought not, I confess to be profan'd
By my poor Muse; nor should an Artless hand
Presume to take a crayon up, to trace
But the faint landscape of so brave a place
Yet noble, Chatsworth, for I speak of thee,
Pardon the love will prompt the injury
My pen must do thee, when, before I end,
I six dishonour, where I could commend."

CHATSWORTH HOUSE

4

POOLE'S CAVERN, BUXTON.

The cavern lies on the southern side of Buxton on Green Lane, and is open to the public. Inside the cave system, which extends 1,800 feet, Romano-British animal remains have been found. The name of the cavern comes from an outlaw named Poole who used the cavern as his base and stronghold for his stolen treasures.

"The first of these I meet with in my way,
Is a vast cave, which the old people say
One Poole an outlaw made his residence;
But why he did so, or for what offence,
The Beagles of the law should press so near,
As, spight of Horrors self, to earth him there,
Is in our times a riddle; and in this
Tradition most unkindly silent is;
But what foe're his crime, than such a cave
A worse imprisonment he could not have . . ."

"A candle, left on purpose at the brook,
On which, with trembling horror, whilst you look,
You'll fancy't from that dreadful precipice,
A spark ascending from the black abyss.
Returning on your road, you thence must still
Higher and higher mount the dangerous hill,
Till, at the last, dirty and tired enough,
Your giddy heads do touch the sparkling roof.
And now you here a while to pant may sir,
To which adventures have thought requisit
To add a bottle, to express the love
They owe their friends left in the world above . . ."

"Then once more through the narrow passage strain,
And you shall see the cheerful day again;
When after two hours darkness, you will say
The sun appears dreft in a brighter ray:
Thus after long restraint, when once set free,
Men better taste the Air of Liberty . . ."

ST. ANNE'S WELL

ST. ANNE'S WELL, BUXTON.

Buxton has long been renowned for its spa water and curative powers. It was not until the 19th Century that the town became a fashionable spa.

"Six hundred paces hence and northward still,
On the descent of such a little hill,
As by the rest of greater bulk, and fame,
Environ'd round, scarcely deserves that name,
A crystal fountain springs in healing streams
Hot, though close shaded from the sun's warm beams,
By a malicious roof, that covers it.
Hither the sick, the lame and the Barren come,
And hence go healthful, Sound and fruitful home . . ."

The spa water, which comes from about a mile underground, is at a constant temperature of 82 degrees Fahrenheit both winter and summer. The water also flows at a constant rate of 200,000 gallons per day. Much of the water is now used in the new swimming baths in the Pavilion Gardens. The water is blue in colour and has resulted in the fact that Buxton is often referred to as the "Spa of Blue Waters". One of the most famous visitors to the Buxton Spa to take the waters was Mary, Queen of Scots. She last came here in 1584 and before she left, as though she already knew her fate, she scratched the following two lines in Latin on a window pane at the Hall. (This is now the Old Hall Hotel on the left-hand side of the Crescent. The building was rebuilt in the 17th Century.)

"Buxton, whose fame thy mild-warm waters tell,
Whom I, perhaps, no more shall see, farewell!"

6

EBBING AND FLOWING WELL, TIDESWELL

EBBING AND FLOWING WELL, TIDESWELL.

Although the name of Tideswell suggests a tiding well, from its ebbing and flowing well, the name in fact derives from a Saxon named Tidi who built a wall, hence Tidiswall. The well is situated in the garden of Craven House at the north western corner of the village. The well, which was a natural syphon, has ceased to ebb and flow since 1790, when new pipes were laid in the road opposite. Cotton came here eleven times before he actually saw it ebb and flow.

"There creeps a Spring that makes a little rill,
Which at first sight to curious visitors,
So small, and so contemptible appears,
They'd think themselves abus'd, did they not stay
To see wherein the wonder of it lay.
This fountain is so very very small,
The observer hardly can perceive it crawl
Through the sedg, which scarcely in their beds
Confess a current by their waving head . . ."

"For now and then, a hollow murmuring sound,
Being first heard remotely underground,
The spring immediately swells and straight
Boils up through several pores to such a height,
As, overflowing soon the narrow shoar,
Below does in a little torrent roar . . ."

ELDON HOLE (1½ miles north of Peak Forest)

The most awesome and yet the most interesting feature of the Derbyshire landscape. Hutchinson wrote in his "Tour through the High Peak of Derbyshire", which was published in 1809, the following:-

> "Eldon Hole, about three miles further, is a dreadful chasm, about ten yards broad and eighteen long, with a depth not positively ascertained. Dr. Plot, who endeavoured to fathom it, says that having let down 2,800 fathoms (16,800 feet!) of line he did not find any bottom, nor the least appearance of water. Some years ago, a cruel wretch confessed at the gallows that he had robbed a poor traveller, and afterwards thrown him into this pit. It is unnecessary to describe my emotions on looking down — the ivy clings to the rocks beneath, and has a most singular appearance."

The actual depth of the hole was for centuries a mystery. Cotton lowered a line down and found it to be 884 yards deep and the last eighty yards of the line was in water. Earlier than Cotton, in Queen Elizabeth's reign, the Earl of Leicester had a man lowered down on a rope. When the man was brought to the surface, he remained silent and died eight days later. A cat has been let down, and this likewise died soon after its return to the surface. On another occasion, a goose was thrown down and it appeared several days later at Peak Cavern, two miles away, completely featherless, as though "singed by the fire of Hell". It has been proved that by putting dye in the water in the bottom the dyed water comes out of Peak Cavern, approximately forty-eight hours later. In about 1755 a farmer was losing a number of cattle, which fell into the hole. He decided to fill the hole up and, with several people helping, they worked away for three days but realised that they were making no impression at all and so gave up. At one time the surrounding wall, which does not exist today, had a life expectancy of seven years. This was because the people who came to visit the hole always dropped a stone down to hear the startling sounds which came from the bowels of the earth. Today the actual depth is known — 245 feet. In the guide book to Derbyshire caves and potholes is the following sentence concerning Eldon Hole. "From the bottom of shaft, cavern is reached through timbered passage, intermittently blocked by decaying cows and sheep."!

Cotton writes on his visit and attempts to fathom its depth.

"But I myself, with half the Peak surrounded,
Eight hundred, four score and four yards have sounded;
And though of these fourscore returned back wet,
The plummet drew and found no bottom yet;
Though when I went to make a new essay,
I could not get the lead down half the way.
This yawning mouth is thirty paces long,
Scarce half so wide, within lin'd through with strong
Continuous walls of solid perpend stone:
A gulf wide, steep, black and a dreadful one;
Which few, that comes to see it, dare come near,
And the more daring still approach with fear.
Having with terror, here beheld a space
The gastly aspect of this dangerous place;
Critical passengers usually found,
How deep the threatening gulf goes under-ground
By tumbling down stones sought throughout the field,
As great as the officious boores can wield."

MAM TOR

The east face of Mam Tor is a banded mass of millstone grit and shale, and is renowned for its instability, hence the nickname "Shivering Mountain". There are several rock climbs up this face. In the summer it is an alarming ascent for everything is very loose. In the winter the rock is frozen together and, although still an exciting climb, it is safer. Around the summit plateau is the single ditch of an Iron Age fort. When Cotton was here he witnessed a local wager, that a man could not climb the face.

"That hands and feet were ready held to quit,
And to feel their Master's fate submit.
How to advance a step he could not tell,
And to descend was as impossible . . .
For to the spectators wonder, and his own,
He panting gained at last the mountain crown."

PEAK CAVERN

In old engravings of Castleton, Peak Cavern is referred to as the "Devil's Arse". The water that runs out of the entrance is said to be the Devil relieving himself! The cavern entrance is the largest in Britain and the second largest in the world. When Cotton was there the entrance was occupied by the rope making families. The rope making apparatus is still there and was used by Mr. H. Marrison, the last of a very long line of rope makers. In 1794 it is recorded that there was a public house under the cavern roof. Two women known as Betty Blewit and Sall Waugh lived in a mud hut under the roof and it was said that they "lived in a house on which the sun never shone nor the rain ever fell". Smoke smut from the chimneys of the house can still be seen on the cavern roof.

"Under this house yawns a dreadful cave,
Whose sight may well astonish the most brave,
And make him pause, ere further he proceed
T' explore what in those gloomy vaults lie hid."

"Now to the cave we come, wherein is found
A new strange thing, a village underground;
Houses and barns for men, and beasts behoof,
With distinct walls, under one solid roof,
Stacks both of hay and turf, which yields a scent
Can only fume from Satan's fundament;
For this black cave lives in the voice of Fame
To the fame sense by a yet corner name."

"The subterrean people ready stand,
A candle each, most two in either hand
To guide, who are to penetrate inclin'd."

"We now begin to travel into night,
Hoping indeed to see the sun again,
Though none of us can tell, or how, or when."

CHATSWORTH HOUSE

"There stands a stately and stupendous pile."

That Chatsworth, Cotton was talking about above, was the house built by Bess of Hardwick in 1572 at a cost of approximately £60,000. It was not until the 1690s that the first Duke of Devonshire began building the Chatsworth we know and admire so much today. The actual building took about 160 years to bring it to today's completeness and occupied much of the time of several Dukes of Devonshire. Of the Elizabethan Chatsworth, little remains; Queen Mary's Bower and the Shooting Lodge above the house are the sole survivors.

LOVER'S LEAPS OF DERBYSHIRE

In the mid 18th Century there was a 'craze' amongst distraught lovers to terminate their lives by throwing themselves off a high limestone cliff. There are four such places in Derbyshire which tradition claims to be Lover's Leaps: at Buxton, Stoney Middleton, Winster and Dovedale. James Croston in his book "On Foot through the Peak" mentions another at Matlock, but despite extensive research I have found no other mention of one there.

BUXTON'S LOVERS LEAP

BUXTON

Marked on the Ordnance Survey map, on the eastern outskirts of Buxton, at Grid Reference SK072727, is this Lover's Leap across a deep limestone gorge. Living in Buxton in the early half of the 18th Century were a young couple who were ardent lovers. Unfortunately, their parents disapproved of the match and did their utmost to discourage the young couple. At length the lovers decided the only solution was to run away and marry at Peak Forest, the 'Gretna Green' of Derbyshire. Around midnight, one night they met and together set off on horseback for Peak Forest. They had not ridden far when they discovered their parents in hot pursuit. Near the limestone gorge, the girl's horse cast a shoe and she leapt onto her lover's horse to continue their journey. At the gorge, without hesitating, they leapt across the deep chasm and carried on. Meanwhile their parents reached the gorge and stopped, for none would dare attempt the leap. The parents returned home and the young couple reached Peak Forest, were wed and rode on southwards. Where, it is said, they lived happily ever after.

STONEY MIDDLETON LOVERS LEAP

STONEY MIDDLETON

Middleton Dale is adorned with steep vertical limestone walls, and it was from the top of one of these that Hannah Bradley, one of the village's beauties, jumped in 1762. Hannah was evidently courted by William Barnsley and for a year they could be seen in the neighbourhood, wandering around enrapt in their love. After about a year, for some unknown reason, William stopped courting Hannah, who was naturally distraught at this turn in her affairs. For a whole week she wandered around in the deepest gloom until finally she could not stand it any more. She decided that the best thing to do was to end her life. The following day she walked to the summit of the limestone cliffs, placed her bonnet and gloves in a hawthorn tree and walked to the lip of the cliff and cried out the following:-

"Oh! my William! my William — false William — no, I will
not call thee false! My love! My life! Never, never
again will mine eyes behold thee! — thee whom I loved -
ah! I love thee still! Oh! my love, wilt thou not come
to my grave, and shed one tear to the memory of her, who
died for thee? I'll bless thee again my love and then
from this dizzy height I'll cast myself and prove to thee
and the world — my love is stronger than death! I sink!
I go, my love, my love!"

She then jumped! Unfortunately her dress, which was made of a heavy coarse material as well as being voluminous, simply mushroomed out and acted as a parachute. On landing she was injured and had to be carried home by friends. What became of William we do not know. Hannah died two years later on 12th December 1764 at the age of 26. Today, at the bottom of the cliffs, is Lover's Leap Cafe sporting a new sign depicting the tragic story.

WINSTER HALL

Dominating the main street of the picturesque village of Winster is the five-bayed, three-storey high Hall. Here in the 18th Century the building was witness to a young couple's leap. The young, beautiful daughter of the household was deeply in love with the coachman. Despite her entreaties her parents strongly disapproved of the match on the grounds of social status. Her parents, to resolve the matter, went ahead with their plan that she should marry someone of their class. The man in question, although admirably suitable, was not their daughter's idea of a lifelong companion. She was totally against the match because she knew she could never love him. On the eve of her wedding she and the coachman climbed to the top of the Hall. After professing their deepest love for each other, they jumped clasped in each other's arms. Both were killed, as they had planned, from the fall. It is said that, for a long while after, the ghost of the daughter was occasionally seen in the forecourt of the Hall.

DOVEDALE

DOVEDALE — BASE OF LOVER'S LEAP

Towards the southern end of Dovedale is this Lover's Leap, marked on the 1″ O.S. Map at Grid Reference SK146517. It is said to be so named because a young maiden who had been jilted by her lover jumped from here hoping to terminate her life. The river Dove flows some 120 feet below. Unfortunately, the numerous bushes at the bottom near the river broke her fall. Instead of ending her life she was able to walk away! From that moment onwards she never thought about her ex-lover again and is reputed to have lived happily, though single, ever after.

THE HOMES OF FAIRIES

There are several places in Derbyshire where fairies, goblins, elves and the little people are known to have lived. Many bear the name Hob Hurst.

A hob hurst was a capricious wood elf, hurst being an old English word for a wood or forest. When in good humour he made everything on the farm, particularly in the dairy, run smoothly and prosper. The cows would give plenty of milk, the cream would churn quickly into butter, and the quantity of hay would increase. But when irritated he would make the cows go dry, the milk turn sour, the crocks smash, and generally infuse a spirit of contrariness into everything.

If Hob was in a bad mood and the person's farm was in confusion, the following charm was spoken to keep Hob away:

> 'Churn, butter, churn!
> Peter stands at the gate
> Waiting for a butter cake!
> Churn, butter, churn!

In Deep Dale, four miles east of Buxton, is Thirst House Cave, which is sometimes known as Hob Hurst House. Here potholers can explore some 200 feet of passageways. In the cave used to live a fairy who was the guardian of the nearby spring. It is said that if you drink from the spring on Good Friday, the water will cure you of any disease. In the nineteenth century, Deep Dale was known as the place to see fairies. On one occasion a man was on his way to Chelmorton and, seeing a fairy, he stealthily crept up and caught him. He put the fairy in his pack and carried on. Unfortunately the fairy created such a noise that the man had no option but to release the fairy, who ran back to the cave.

In Monsal Dale, on the western slopes of Finn Cop, is another cave among a group of shattered limestone pinnacles. Here again a fairy is supposed to have lived, and the position is marked on the 1:25,000 Ordnance Survey map as Hob Hurst House. A verse about the area states:

> 'The Piper of Shacklow,
> The fiddler of Finn,
> The old woman of Demon's Dale,
> Calls them all in.'

All the names refer to places thereabouts. Demon's Dale is on the eastern side of Deep Dale (a different one from that near Buxton). Here on the field in front of Demon Dale is where witches are supposed to have danced.

Above Chatsworth Park is Brampton East Moor, and at its southern end is another Hob Hurst House. In fact it is a Bronze Age burial mound, but it is the reputed home of a goblin.

In the upper regions of the River Dove and near the Derbyshire-Staffordshire boundary is a marshy piece of ground, where 'boggarts' are seen. The 'boggarts' are said to be the spirits of dead travellers who have lost their way and been sucked down by the marshy ground. On several occasions a flickering light has been seen dancing over the area, which has terrified the locals and kept them indoors at night.

TWO FAIRY TALES

Both tales come from the northern half of the Peak District, and the first one was frequently told in Eyam.

A farmer's wife, having made a pudding, placed it in a pan of water on the fire to boil it. Soon after the water had boiled, the pudding began jumping about in the pan and eventually jumped straight out and rolled around the floor, as though possessed of a spirit. While this was going on, a tinker knocked at the door. The farmer's wife answered the door and, seeing who it was, gave the tinker the pudding. The tinker left, delighted with his gift, and placed the pudding in his knapsack. He had not gone far before the pudding began jumping up and down in his knapsack. He stopped, took off the sack, undid the flap and removed the pudding. It continued jumping about until it broke, and a fairy child stepped out and said, 'Take me to my dathera dad, take me to my dathera dad.'

The other tale concerns a Methodist minister who lost his way on the moors. Eventually he came to a house where he was invited to stay for the night. However, they warned him that unexpected things might happen during the night. The minister was so tired that he went to bed without eating anything. In the early hours of the morning he was awakened by the sound of movement downstairs and of pots being laid on the table. Moments later he heard footsteps up the stairs followed by a knock on the door. A voice called, 'Armaleg, come to thy supper'. He dressed quickly and did as bidden, and went down to supper. On entering the dining room he was amazed to see the room crowded with people and a huge pile of food on the table. Before he could eat, he said grace, which included the words, 'Devils, fear and fly.'. When he opened his eyes again, the room was empty and the table was bare.

HOW TO CHOOSE A SERVANT

The following tale comes from North Derbyshire. A farmer's wife was wanting to engage a maid servant, and consequently several girls applied for the position. Each was to come at a different time for an interview, and the man-servant suggested a little test for them all. The farmer's wife agreed to his suggestion, and a besom, which is a brush made of twigs, was laid across the path up which the applicants would walk to the house.

From the window, the farmer's wife and the man-servant watched. The first one came, and on reaching the broom she kicked it to one side, to which they agreed, 'She's an idle slut, and can't bend her back.' When the second one came, she simply jumped over the broom. 'She won't do; she'll skip her work.' was the verdict, and therefore she was not employed. The third approached, and on reaching the broom she picked it up and placed it in a corner. The farmer's wife remarked, 'That's the girl for me; she'll be careful, industrious and tidy.'. She was appointed.

DOCTOR'S GATE

Bisecting the two peat moorland masses of Kinder and Bleaklow in North Derbyshire is a Roman road known as Doctor's Gate. The road links the Roman forts of Melandra in Glossop with Navio at Brough in the Hope Valley. The road is frequently named the 'High Street of the Peak'. Although the road was constructed by Romans in about A.D. 78, how it became known as Doctor's Gate is a mystery, but perhaps the following legend explains.

In nearby Hayfield, near Glossop, lived a local magician. His fame spread, and he later became known as Dr. Faust after the celebrated sixteenth century Dr. Faust from Germany. One day the Devil paid him a visit and, during the conversation, the magician challenged him to a horse-race. The Devil laughed aloud, for everyone knew he had the fastest horse in the kingdom. However, the magician was persistent and the Devil agreed. The arrangements of the race, which was to follow the line of the old Roman road, were settled. The Devil was to allow the magician a good lead, and was to have his freedom if he won, but, if the doctor lost, the Devil bargained, 'On a day which I shall name, thou shalt wait upon me and deliver up thy soul to me.'. The magician agreed to these daunting conditions.

When the day of the race came, the Devil, as agreed, allowed the magician a very large start; in fact larger than he intended, for he was feeling over-confident. At last the Devil set off at a whirlwind pace and caught the magician up, just as he was about to disappear from view. The Devil, instead of passing the magician, decided on some fun, and so drew level and tugged the magician's horse's tail. Although intended to slow the other horse down, this had the reverse effect, for the horse galloped harder. As the Devil enjoyed his game he was unaware of what they were approaching. Before he could do anything to avert disaster, they both crossed a stream of water. Whereupon the Devil lost immediately, for one of the laws of sorcery states that, when a person is pursued by the Devil and they cross a running stream, the Devil loses all power over him. The Devil admitted defeat, but was furious, and to show his annoyance he scratched a long gash in the moorland, which is known today as Devil's Dyke. The magician rode home victorious, and the Devil rode humbly home.

DOCTOR'S GATE, ROMAN ROAD

THE MERMAID'S POOL

'Where the dreadful Downfall casts its awful shade,
In a deep glen which rifted rocks have made,
Whose towering cliffs seem bury'd in the skies,
The Mermaid Pool a weedy bog now lies.
Tradition tells us, that in times that have been
The pool was deep, its banks around were green,
And on an Easter Sunday morning there
The same which comes once every year;
Just when the earthy dawn broke o'er the hills,
And shed grey twilight o'er the gloomy vales,
The Mermaid might be seen, (like nymphs of old,
which poets feign'd or superstition told).
Woman, and fish, so strangely blent in one,
So fables tell, and so, old legends run.
Now on the velvet bank in sportive play;
And when prevailed the part of woman fair,
Into long flowing locks it curl'd its hair,
Breathes the swift zephyrs as they gently rise,
And its fair bosom heaves with human sighs;
But when the fish prevails beneath the tides,
Like lightning it a scaley monster glides;
And in its wat'ry cavern must remain,
Till Easter Sunday morning comes again.'.

'The Mermaid Pool, Kinder' by H. Redfern

MERMAID'S POOL

The Mermaid's Pool, large and serene, lies on the western side of Kinder Scout, just below
Kinder Downfall. As the legend in the old poem above claims, people visiting the pool in the
early morning of Easter Sunday can see a Mermaid. It is reputed that those who see her gain
everlasting life. In the nineteenth century the people of Hayfield, the town nearby, firmly
believed this. No one has ever been known to actually confirm that he or she has physically
seen her. One person from Hayfield, Aaron Ashton, went to the pool every Easter Sunday, but
he too never commented on his visits. We are left to conjecture, for he died aged 104 in 1835.

Another version of the legend states that the mermaid lures the watching males into the pool.
If the person refuses to come into the pool with her, she drags you in to your death. It is said
that several people have been drowned because of this.

HAYFIELD GHOSTS

I have found two snippets of stories connecting Hayfield with ghosts. In the sixteenth century in the cemetery of a small chapel all the dead are said to have risen from their graves, clothed in gold.

Close to Highgate Hall, which lies about half a mile south east of Hayfield, is a sealed well. Apparently a Scottish pedlar was murdered near it, and his bones were found in a nearby garden and were reinterred in Hayfield churchyard about 1770. As long as the well remains sealed, the ghost of the pedlar will not haunt the area.

YOUNGATE BRIDGE

JACOB'S LADDER

One of the ways of ascending Kinder Scout is by Jacob's Ladder, which also forms part of the alternative route of the Pennine Way. Situated at Grid Reference SK087863 is this short but steep climb. Living at Youngit Farm in Upper Edale in the 1820's was Jacob Marshall. He earned a living by transporting goods to and from the village by pack-horse, and regularly crossed from Edale via Edale Cross to Hayfield and onto Stockport. He often carried the wool for sale to Stockport and never came back empty, bringing the supplies for the farmers on his return journey. The bridge at the bottom of Jacob's Ladder, across the infant Noe, is known as Youngate Bridge. When Jacob had crossed the river, he made his donkeys take the gentle path up on the left, while he ascended direct. He always carried a spade, and made a step or two each crossing, completing in the end his own 'ladder' up the valley side.

LORD'S SEAT

Nearly a mile due west of Mam Tor on Rushup Edge (Grid Reference SK114835) is Lord's Seat. This is believed to be so named because William Peveril (a major landowner in Derbyshire in the twelfth century, including Peveril Castle, Castleton; Haddon Hall; and Bolsover Castle) and his successors came to sit here, while they watched the chase or hunt for both deer and wild boar.

Another Lord's Seat can be found close to Stanage Edge and the above story is told about this spot as well. However, this second seat located half a mile north east of Stanage Pole, was also a farm. Non-conformists are said to have met in this building between 1662 and 1700. In 1664 the Coventide Act was passed prohibiting private religious worship of five or more people. Despite this they met regularly, knowing that the punishment, if they were caught, was as follows:-

1st Offence — £5 fine or three months in gaol.
2nd Offence — £10 fine or six months in gaol.
3rd Offence — £100 fine or seven years' transportation.

MURDER STONE

THE MURDER STONE

'William Wood
Eyam, Derbyshire
Here
Murdered
16th July
A.D. 1823
Prepare to meet thy God.'

On the minor road from Whaley Bridge to Disley on the eastern slopes of Black Hill, is a stone in the road wall with the above inscription. It is just inside the Derbyshire boundary. The body of William Wood was found by two people, Edmund Pott and John Mellor, who were returning from Stockport to Kettleshulme where they lived. They came across William's body, still warm, lying in the gutter, and it was evident that he had been battered to death. The two of them picked up the body and, with several stones as evidence, they loaded him into their cart and set off for Whaley Bridge. Here the body was left in the Cock Inn for the coroner.

At the enquiry the following Saturday, it was learnt that William was aged thirty and left a widow with three children. He had been to Manchester to sell cloth, for which he had received a bill of exchange for £60 plus £10 in notes. He had changed the bill of exchange in Stockport, and the cashier had made a note of the numbers, as had been done in Manchester with the £10. This was most fortuitous, as it made it possible to trace the murderers. Witnesses at the enquiry were able to state that they had seen William walking along followed at a distance by three young men.

The day after the murder several of the notes were exchanged in Macclesfield, and this led to the arrest of Charles Taylor on July 18th. He knew his fate was bad and tried to commit suicide, but unfortunately the attempt failed, although he badly injured himself and died later. Before he died he related what had happened.

Three young men had met William by chance in Chapel-en-le-Frith, and he had invited them into a nearby inn for a drink. While they were drinking they learned that he had a large sum of money on him. Later they parted company and met William further up the road where they battered him to death, took the money and left. Taylor also informed that the other two were named Dale and Platt. Dale was arrested on August 9th, went for trial at Chester Assizes and was executed on April 21, 1824, at Chester City Gaol. Platt was never caught.

DICKEY O'TUNSTEAD — A RESTLESS SKULL

But the head of Ned Dickson still stood in the nook,
Though they tried to remove it by bell and by book;
Though wasted of skin and of flesh, still the skull
Will remain at its post till it's weird by full.

William Bennett

For over 350 years a skull known as Dickey o'Tunstead has played a vital part in the occupier's life at Tunstead Farm on the west side of Combs reservoir, near Chapel-en-le-Frith. The skull, although named as male, is believed in fact to be a female's. For many years the skull was kept in front of a small window at the bottom of the stairs and strongly objected to being disturbed. The window behind always had a pane of glass missing, so that the skull could breathe. Glass had been fitted into the gap, but the next day it was always found to be broken.

Recently the skull was permanently bricked into the house wall. Whose the skull was is unknown, but there is a tradition that at one time two co-heiresses were living there. One was murdered, and just before she expired she gasped that her bones would stay there for ever. Some of the popular stories about the skull follow.

The skull leaves everyone in peace and does not cause any trouble. In fact she is rather helpful, as we shall see. However, if the skull is moved, all manner of events take place. On two occasions the skull has been buried in the churchyard at Chapel-en-le-Frith. Each time this has happened, 'There has been weeping and wailing, gnashing of teeth, furniture thrown about and cattle strayed and died.' Naturally, the owner has quickly exhumed the skull, put it back on the window-sill, and once more peace has reigned.

On another occasion the house was being rebuilt and the skull was gaily thrown outside. The workmen engaged on the building returned each morning, only to find that their previous day's work had been damaged. As they hammered a low moan could be heard coming from the ground. Once the skull was put back, everything was normal. When the London and North Western Railway was being constructed, part of it was planned to cross the farmland of Tunstead. Work was started, and even a bridge was built. The work was continually hampered, and when the bridge mysteriously sank the work was abandoned and the line was constructed further away. This accounts for the large curve at this point in the line.

The skull had its good side, for if a cow was calving during the night the skull would rouse the owner. Likewise if any cattle strayed. If the servants wanted to be up early in the morning, Dickey would awaken them. The same applied to the horses, and they were often found with their saddles on, waiting. Finally, if any relation or personal friend was to die soon, Dickey would always give advance warning.

One owner of the farm in the nineteenth century is recorded as saying that the skull prevented his house from being robbed, and that he would far sooner lose his best cow than the skull.

COMBS RESERVOIR

THE BLACK HOLE OF DERBYSHIRE

The church of Chapel-en-le-Frith stands on the site known as the Black Hole of Derbyshire. In 1648 the Scots, under the leadership of the Duke of Hamilton, came down into England to help Charles the First. The army was defeated by Cromwell at Preston, and 1,500 Scots were taken prisoner and eventually brought to Chapel-en-le-Frith a month later. Here they were locked into the small church, which was far too small to house such a large number. Between September 14th and 30th they remained locked inside. When the doors were opened, forty four of them were found to be dead. The Scots were immediately made to march to Chester, and before covering a few miles many more had collapsed and died.

CHAPEL EN LE FRITH CHURCH

23

STADEN LOW

Staden Low is situated about one and a half miles south east of Buxton at Grid Reference SK072723. At the beginning of the last century, it was written that 'The officers of the surrounding hamlets have, in consequence of some ancient prescription, till within these few years been annually chosen on the top of Staden Low (and their names registered in the parochial records) on a large flat stone placed there for the purpose, and which has, time immemorial, occupied that situation.'.

BEN STILES' GHOST

Lying two and a half miles due south of Buxton, and just south west of Harpur Hill, at Grid Reference SK055697, is a solitary building known as The Firth. It is recorded that in about 1800 a person named Ben was murdered here and that his body was found beside a stile; hence his nickname, Ben Stiles. It is said that his ghost haunts this area, and can be seen by privileged people only, between sunset and sunrise.

THE QUIET WOMAN

On the western edge of Derbyshire, some four miles south of Buxton, is the small limestone village of Earl Sterndale. The inn there is called 'The Quiet Woman'. The inn sign depicts a woman in a long dress but with her head missing. The motto underneath records, 'Soft words turneth away wrath.'. There are two stories of how the inn received its name.

The first records that the landlady was a regular chatterbox. Her husband's life was miserable, but he struggled on. Eventually he could stand her voice no more, for not only had he to contend with it during the day, but she had begun to talk in her sleep. He was now at his wit's end, and so cut off her head. The villagers were all glad that this had been done, for their lives were made equally miserable by her constant tongue. The villagers collected money betwen them and purchased a gravestone which bore an epitaph warning other chatter-boxes. The remaining money was given to the landlord.

The other explanation, which is totally different, records that every market day the landlord went to Longnor Market, two miles away. He was a man of routine who always returned home at the same time each week. Following one market he was delayed. His wife, wondering what had happened, sent someone to look for him. When her husband finally arrived, she was most angry at him for being late. He was likewise angry at her that she had sent someone to look for him. As a result they had a really good row. In the end the landlord walked out and said, 'If I can't have a quiet woman inside, I will have a quiet woman outside.', and had the inn sign painted.

TIP'S GRAVE

IN MEMORY OF TIP

Beside the western edge of Howden Reservoir is a stone memorial to the dog Tip. The monument was unveiled on April 30, 1955, to record for posterity a simple story of devotion. On December 12, 1953, Joseph Wragg, who lived near the Yorkshire Bridge at Bamford, set off with his bitch collie, Tip, for a walk to the Howden Moors. It was not until fifteen weeks later, on March 27, 1954, that both were seen again. The winter was a bad one, and as soon as it was known that Mr. Wragg had not returned, search parties were organised but no trace was found. It was on that March day that Mr. Sam Bingham was walking on the moor when he suddenly saw something move. He walked over to investigate and found the body of Mr. Wragg, and his faithful dog Tip, who although very weak was still keeping vigil over his master's corpse.

The full story of such devotion became headline news. The dog was taken to Mr. Wragg's niece, Mrs. Thorp, and she nursed the dog back to health and made a home for her in their household. To this day no-one knows how the dog survived through those fifteen weeks of winter in such a bleak location. At the Bamford Sheepdog Trials on Whit Monday 1954, Tip was presented with the bronze medal of the National Canine Defence League. Also at the trials a 'Tribute to Tip Fund' was launched. This resulted in sufficient money being raised to purchase a monument and erect it near her vigil. Regrettably, Tip died before the monument was unveiled on February 16, 1955, but was buried on the moors near to the spot where she had stayed beside her master.

It is a touching tale and one of Derbyshire's newest legends, but one that deserves to become immortal.

TWO SUBMERGED VILLAGES

Lying under the water of Ladybower reservoir are the villages of Derwent and Ashopton. The reservoir is the third and last of the valley, and work began on its construction in 1935; it was officially opened in 1945. Of the other two reservoirs, Howden, the uppermost one, was built in 1912 and Derwent was completed in 1916. The villages of Derwent and Ashopton were evacuated and the inhabitants rehoused near Bamford. Their houses were knocked down and, when the reservoir was filled, only the solitary spire of the church could be seen. This was later blown up in 1947. During exceptionally dry summers, the reservoir level becomes very low, often exposing the crumbled mounds of the houses of Derwent village. (G.R. SK185886).

The site of Derwent Hall, built by the Balguy family in 1672, lies under the water. In its last years it served as a Youth Hostel, and before it was finally submerged its gate posts were removed, and after being redressed have been re-erected at the entrance to the dam wall. Similarly, the packhorse bridge that used to be here was taken down and has been rebuilt a mile north of Howden reservoir, at Slippery Stones.

There is a tradition that a nobleman was kept secretly at Derwent Hall for many months. Although it has never been proved, it seems probable that this was during 1745, when Bonnie Prince Charles was on his ill-fated manoeuvres. One day the nobleman became ill and a servant, by accident, went into his room and, on seeing his artificial leg beside the bed, she fainted. Once his identity had been revealed, for he was renowned for having lost his leg, he was forced to make a hurried departure and find another place to hide.

Approximately two miles north of the site of Derwent village, and marked on the map, is 'Lost Lad', about half a mile west of Back Tor. According to a legend a young man died leaving his son, aged twelve, to look after his mother and flock of sheep. One year there was a bad snow storm which clothed the area deep in snow. When the snow ceased to fall, his mother told him to go out and round up the sheep. He left the village and began ascending the valley side to Derwent Edge. Finding his sheep, he gathered them together ready for bringing them home. However, he was so involved in his task he was unaware that the weather was deteriorating. Before he knew what was happening, the storm blew up again obliterating his tracks. He wandered for hours until in the dark he found a rock shelter. He crawled inside, and before falling asleep he scratched the words 'Lost Lad' on the rock. That night, because of the intense cold, he died. Despite the efforts of his mother and friends, it was not until three months later that his body was found. Ever since then, passing shepherds have placed a stone on the ever increasing cairn as a monument to this lost boy.

GRAINFOOT'S THREE TREES

Before Ladybower reservoir was filled in 1945, there existed on the right hand side of the valley, under the slopes of Derwent Edge, Grainfoot farm. Today only the gateposts and outer buildings are visible, together with a few yew trees. It is said that the farmer who lived and worked here planted a tree for each of his three sons. Two of his sons had a very full and long life, and their two trees attained a great age. The third son died in India in his middle years, and his tree had stunted growth.

ASHOPTON VIADUCT, LADYBOWER RESERVOIR

CUTTHROAT BRIDGE

Located at Grid Reference SK214874 and lying just east of Ladybower Reservoir on the A57, is Cutthroat Bridge. It takes its name from the following incident:-

> 'Found a man with a wound in his throat in Eashaw
> Clough; he and others, taking him to be of Wormhill,
> Derbyshire, carried him to the house at Lady Bower,
> half a mile from the clough, and then to Bamford Hall,
> where in two days he died.'

In fact the victim was found in Highshaw Clough, which lies some forty yards north east of the bridge, sometime between the years 1587 and 1635.

CUTTHROAT BRIDGE

28

PEVERIL CASTLE

Peveril Castle, which William Peveril started to build in the late eleventh century, was the setting, according to a tradition, of a mediaeval tournament. His daughter Millet refused to wed any ordinary knight, and insisted that suitors must fight for her hand. As a result her father organised a tournament, and many suitors came from far and wide. Their prize was Millet and also Salop Castle. When everyone had assembled the suitors paired and fought each other. The winner was a knight of immense strength and stature named Guarine de Metz. To gain the fair Millet's hand, he had despatched both the King of Scotland's son and the Baron of Burgoyne.

THE CASTLE HOTEL, CASTLETON

This well-known hostelry is reputedly haunted. On several occasions a lady dressed in white has been seen hurrying through the passageways. She is said to be a woman who was jilted by her lover on her wedding day. He never came to the church, and the wedding breakfast to be held in the hotel after the ceremony was abandoned. The lady, who died heart-broken, often walks in the passageways to the dining room where they were supposed to eat. Even in most recent times, ghosts have been seen here. A new landlord in 1960 saw a man in a blue pin-stripe suit, who vanished into thin air. This well-dressed ghost was also seen by several others. It is also claimed that the body of a murdered woman was laid under one of the stone steps here in 1603.

THE EYRES OF HOPE

The Eyre family has been associated with the Hope Valley area for centuries. How they came to live in the Hope valley, and how they received the name Eyre, is explained in the following two legends.

A person named Truelove came across with William the Conqueror. He fought in the Battle of Hastings, October 14, 1066, and during the battle he came to the rescue of William, who had been knocked off his horse. His helmet was restricting his breathing and Truelove removed the helmet. Whereupon Williams asked what his name was. Finding it to be Truelove, William said, 'From now on your name shall be Air, for you have given me air to breathe.'.

Later in the battle, William went to find Eyre, to see what progress he was making. He found Eyre badly injured, to the extent that his leg had to be amputated. William told him that when he was better he would give him some land. Eyre replied, 'I shall call it Hope, for you have given me hope to live.'. Indeed if you inspect the Eyre coat of Arms, in Hope Church, you will see a single leg depicted above the shield.

The other legend states that the Eyres were fighting in the Battle of Win and Lose Hill. During the battle one of the leaders was surrounded by the enemy, and Eyre, who was one of his most faithful supporters, rushed to his aid, killed many of the enemy and rescued his chief. Once in safety the chief turned to Eyre and asked what was his name.

> 'Truelove', he answered.
> The chief replied, 'It shall be Truelove no longer, and
> if we win this battle today, thy name shall be Eyre, and
> thou shalt be 'heir' to the whole of this valley.'.

Later that day the battle was won by the chief, and Eyre was given the valley.

Eyre wanted his loyal friend Fox to share in his good fortune, and therefore made him his steward. Eyre lived at Highlow Hall, which lies in the Hope Valley, about a mile south west of Hathersage. He put his steward, Fox, into a house nearby, which is known as Callow Farm (but not today's structure). It was named Callow because Eyre said,

> 'We'll call this place the Call-o'er, for we'll call thee
> o'er when we want thee.'

It is also said that this Eyre had seven sons, and that he built a Hall for each of them. From his Hall, Highlow, he could see their halls, and by raising a flag could summon just one or all his sons.

The halls were Moorseats, Shatton, Nether Shatton, Hazelford, Offerton, Crookhill and North Lees, and many of them still stand today.

Eyre's steward later built a house at the road junction just above Longshaw Lodge. The building is now a public house and appropriately called Fox House Inn after the original builder, Fox of Callow.

NORTH LEES HALL

BODY SNATCHING

During the nineteenth century there was considerable trade in secretly exhuming recently buried bodies for dissection.

Late at night 'Resurrection carts' came from both Manchester and Sheffield creaked into the Hope Valley on such missions.

The Hope Parish registers contain the following two entries.

1831 October 26th. Aged 28, William Radwell, Smalldale. The body stolen same night.

1834 October 2nd. Aged 21, Benjamin Wragg, Bradwell. This body stolen.

In other counties watch-towers were built near the churchyard to keep a look-out for the body snatchers.

In the churchyard of Bradfield church in South Yorkshire, over the border — but still part of the Peak District National Park — is a watch house built in 1745. (Grid Reference SK267925.)

BRADFIELD WATCH TOWER

THE WEDDING UNDER THE TREE

I cannot locate exactly where the following event took place, but I believe it was somewhere in the northern tip of the county. Although this is the only report I have found of such an incident in Derbyshire there must be other tales, for it seems to have been quite a common occurrence in neighbouring Cheshire.

One wild day two young couples were crossing the fields to a village to be married in the church there. As they walked, the weather deteriorated and, on reaching a large tree, they sheltered underneath it as a storm broke. Moments later they were joined by an Irish priest, who likewise sought shelter from the now furious storm. While the storm raged, the priest noticed that the young couples looked sad, and upon enquiry they said,

'We are all on our way to church to be married, but the storm has
hindered us, and we are afraid it is now too late.'

'If that is all', said the priest, 'I can marry you.'.

Using his prayer book he married them under the branches of the tree while the storm continued. He ended the brief ceremony by saying to each couple individually,

> 'Under a tree in stormy weather
> I married this man and maid together;
> Let him alone who rules the thunder
> Put this man and maid asunder.'.

HOPE CHURCH

32

TWO PEAKLAND WEDDINGS

Married in Wormhill Church was Ann Brightmore, who lived to be 103 years of age. Her father, James Ball, was employed as the gardener at Wormhill Hall, and she was employed as a maid. When it was time for the ceremony she quickly slipped over to the church, from the Hall, with her sweeping brush in her hand. Her husband-to-be was likewise busy, working on the church roof, and he hurried down with his trowel in his hand. Devoted to duty and devoted to each other, they lived happily ever after.

Another old wives' tale tells of a couple who were getting married in Hope Church. They duly arrived and the ceremony began. The couple stood before the vicar but about halfway through the proceedings the bridegroom heard the call of the hounds. He was a very keen huntsman and, leaving everyone, he ran out of the church and joined in the hunt. The ceremony was completed the following day without any further interruption!

Following a Peakland wedding and during the usual high spirits and merry-making, it was quite usual for someone to slip out and fix a bell to the underside of the bed which the newly married couple were to use that night.

BRADWELL

THE BATTLE OF EDWIN TREE, BRADWELL

The inn which stands at the road junction of the minor road from Hope and the B6049, at Grid Reference SK175818, situated just north of Bradwell village, is said to be the site where a king was captured. A battle is believed to have taken place in this area sometime during the Heptarchy, the period of English history from A.D. 449 to 828. A king or chieftain, known as Edwin, was caught here after the battle and was immediately hanged from a tree. The tree has long since disappeared, but was referred to as Edwin's Tree or Edden's Tree. Many of the surrounding names, such as Rebellion Knoll and Gore Lane, give evidence of troublesome times.

THE BRADWELL GHOST

In the eighteenth century there existed in Bradwell a house known as 'Hill's Head' where in about 1760 a young girl was murdered and her body placed in the staircase. Occasionally at first, the girl's ghost would haunt the owners. As time passed the ghost became more of a frequent visitor and was seen both inside and outside the house. In the end the whole neighbourhood became alerted and frightened of going outside at night and meeting the ghost. To end what was becoming a nightmare, everyone agreed that the ghost should be laid.

A person well versed in such practices was brought to the haunted house. Here everyone gathered and watched the exorcist at work. First he drew a chalk ring on the floor before stepping into it and kneeling to pray. He prayed ardently, and beads of sweat began to roll down his face. The floor, according to the onlookers, began to rise and fall. Suddenly the exorcist rose and shouted loudly, 'Beroald, Beroald, Balbin, gab gabor agaba'.
This means, 'Arise! Arise! I charge and command thee!'. The ghost appeared and the exorcist instructed her to retire to Lumb Mouth, another part of the village, where the stream, Bradwell Brook, appears. Here the ghost was to swim about as a fish. The exorcist also told the ghost that on Christmas Day she could turn herself into a white ousel and for exercise could fly to Lumbly Pool, two miles away. From that moment onwards the villagers of Bradwell were left in peace.

HAZLEBADGE HALL

34

THE GHOST OF BRADWELL DALE

Part way through this dale is Hazlebadge Hall. Above the mullioned window can be seen the coat of arms of the Vernon family and the date 1549 below it, which records when the building was constructed. The Hall formed part of the dowry which the fabled Dorothy Vernon brought to her husband, John Manners. Recorded in a book published at the beginning of this century is the following story.

'On any wild night, when the winds howl furiously and the rain falls in torrents, there can be seen in the gorge between Bradwell and Hazelbadge, the spirit of a lady on horseback, the steed rushing madly in the direction of the old Hall. It is said to be the ghost of Margaret Vernon, the last of that line of the Vernons who were living at Hazelbadge for three centuries. She had given her heart, with its fullness of affection, unto the keeping of one who had plighted his troth with another, and when she discovered his treachery she had braced up her nerves to witness his union in Hope Church. But at the finish of the ceremony she had ridden to her home as if pursued by fiends, with eyeballs starting from their sockets, and her brain seized with a fever from which she would never have recovered only from the tender nursing of those around her. Her spirit, they say, on a spectre steed, still rushes madly between Hope and Hazelbadge at midnight.'

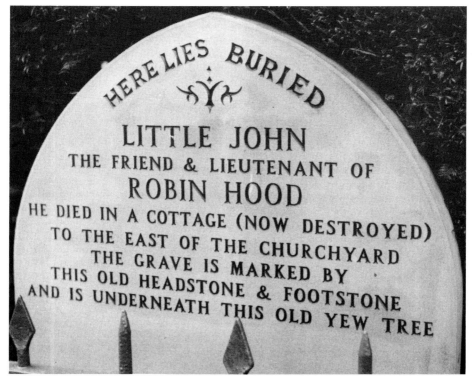

LITTLE JOHN GRAVESTONE

LITTLE JOHN

'His bow was in the chancel hung;
His last good bolt they drave
Down to the rocks, its measured length,
Westward fro' the grave.

And root and bud this shaft put forth
When spring returned anon;
It grew a tree, and threw a shade,
Where slept staunch Little John.'

From an old ballad.

Hathersage is Little John country, the faithful companion of Robin Hood. His name is believed to have been John the Nailor, for he made nails for a living. According to the tradition, Little John fought at the Battle of Evesham in August 1265, under Simon de Montfort. They lost the battle, and everyone escaped fearing for their lives. It is said that for this reason Little John and Robin Hood became outlaws and were 'masters in the virtual sense of the word, of all the country between the Trent and Calder'.

Robin Hood died aged eighty, and was buried 'with his bow in his hand and a green sod under his head and another under his feet' by Little John at Kirklees Priory in Yorkshire. Little John returned to Hathersage and, on gaining the summit of a hill and being able to see his village, he remarked he was approaching the place where he would die. He reached his cottage, which stood to the east of the church, and breathed his last.

His grave, with a modern tombstone, can be seen in the churchyard. In 1784 John Shuttleworth excavated the thirteen and a half feet long grave and found a thigh bone twenty nine and a half inches long. This would make Little John about eight feet tall. It is recorded that in 1652 his long bow, which was five feet long, was hanging in the church. So, too, was his cap by a chain. Both these and the thigh bone were taken to Cannon Hall near Barnsley. Their actual whereabouts today are unknown. Several places in the vicinity of Hathersage bear the name of these renowned outlaws. Two miles north of the village is Robin Hood's Cave on Stanage Edge. Westwards is Robin Hood's Cross on Offerton Moor, and two miles away is Robin Hood's Stoop. The latter is said to be the place where Little John fired an arrow which landed one and a half miles away in the churchyard. Three miles south-east of Hathersage is Little John's Well. There are other wells similarly named, scattered through the county.

HATHERSAGE CHURCH

HATHERSAGE BELL-RINGERS' NOTICE

'You gentlemen that here do wish to ring,
See that these laws ye keep in ev'ry thing
Or else be sure, you must without delay
The penalty thereof to the ringers pay.
First when ye do into the bell-house come,
Look if the ringers have convenient room;
For if ye be an hindrance unto them
Fourpence ye forfeit to these gentlemen.
Next if ye do intend, here for to ring
With hat or spurs on do not touch a string:
For if you do, your forfeit is for that
Just fourpence, or else you lose your hat.
If you a bell turn o'er, without delay
Fourpence unto the ringers you must pay.
Or if you strike, miscall, or do abuse
You must pay fourpence for the ringers' use.
For every oath here sworn, ere you go hence
Unto the poor you must pay twelvepence;
And if that you desire to be enrolled
A ringer here, these orders keep and hold;
But whoso doth these orders disobey
Unto the stocks we'll take him straightaway;
There to remain until that he be willing
To pay the forfeit and the clerk a shilling.'

A copy of this notice is still kept in the tower. The stocks were near the main entrance to the churchyard, but sadly these were removed years ago.

PRESERVED BODIES

The moorland areas around Hope and Hathersage are renowned for their preserving qualities, as the two following accounts bear witness.

A grazier named Barber and his maid-servant were on their way to Ireland in January 1764. They lost their way in a snowstorm, and it was not until May when the snow melted that the bodies were discovered. The coroner ordered that they were to be buried where they were found. A shallow grave about three feet deep was dug. Twenty years later the bodies were uncovered and found — 'the colour of the skin being fair and natural, and their flesh as soft as that of persons newly dead'. Over the next twenty years the grave was frequently opened and the bodies began to decay. In 1816 Mr. Henry Brown, M.D. of Chesterfield, inspected the couple and found the man with 'his beard strong and about a quarter of an inch long: the hair of his head short — his skin hard and of a tanned colour'. He found the woman was more decayed. Later, the man's grandson, Mr. Barber of Rotherham, had the bodies exhumed in the presence of the Rev. Wermald, the vicar of Hope. They were taken to Hope and buried in the churchyard. Later the grave was opened and both were found to be in a very decayed state.

A similarly preserved body was found in Hathersage churchyard in 1781. Henry Ibbotson wrote from Carrhead, Hathersage on December 9, 1789, the following:

'Dear Sir,

By your request, I send you as particular account as possible relating to the corpse of Mr. Benjamin Ashton; he was interr'd the 29th December, 1725, in the 42nd year of his age (very corpulent) and was taken up 31st May, 1781. His coffin was of oak boards, one and a half inches thick, and as sound as when laid in the ground; as they laid over head in water, men were set to work to lade water all night for to keep it down while the corpse was laid in the ground again. The coffin being opened, his body was found entirely in the same posture as when laid in, only with this difference, that it was congealed as hard as flint. His breast, belly and face were swarthy, but, when turned over, his back and all the parts that lay under was nearly of the same colour as when put into the coffin at first. His head was broke off with taking out of the coffin, but was put in again as near the same posture as possible. This is as minute account as I can give you.

From your obedient humble servant,

Henry Ibbotson.

Sent to Mr. N.C. of Edale.

THE GABRIEL HOUNDS

Recorded in William Wood's book, TALES AND TRADITIONS OF THE HIGH PEAK, is the following legend concerning Gabriel Hounds. In the eighteenth and nineteenth centuries, the sound of a howling hound was fervently believed to be an omen of coming death. In fact, the dog-like sound was made by a bird.

Living in a quiet dale near Hathersage were the Bowmans. Mary Bowman was said to be one of the most attractive girls of the area, and was being courted by a local man named Birch. In due course they wished to marry, but her father was against the idea, for he believed that she would be marrying beneath herself. Not long afterwards her father was informed by his employer that a friend of his would be coming for a week's shooting and suggested that he could stay at his house. Mr. Bowman replied by return, saying that his guest was most welcome. The guest, Mr.Galliard, arrived a few days later, and everyone was enchanted by his appearance. Mary remained faithful to Birch and avoided Mr. Galliard whenever possible, but, from their brief encounters, Mr. Galliard developed a strong liking for Mary. As a result, he stayed and tried to woo her.

The situation was becoming very awkward and Mary, Birch and her brother devised a plan. A few days later Mary fell ill and was confined to bed. The days passed and instead of getting better she grew worse. One evening, two weeks after she first went to bed, the sound of a Gabriel Hound was heard. 'My God', said Mrs. Bowman, 'tis the Gabriel Hound, death is in our dwelling.' The sound was heard three times, and Mr. Bowman remarked, 'Ah! This death token — I never knew it fail — my Mary, thy doom is sealed!' Up to this time Mr. Galliard had remained constantly at her bedside hoping for a miracle. But alas, having heard the Gabriel Hound, he knew this was not possible. The next morning, heavy-hearted, he left with Mr. Bowman. When Mr. Bowman returned he was met by his wife, who said, 'She is gone, my Mary!' Mr. Bowman thought she had died, but instead Mary had leapt out of bed and run to Birch at an agreed rendezvous. From here they rode to a church and were married. The sound of the hound had been made by Birch!

WHISPERING ALOUD

A young girl who regularly saw her boyfriend, suggested that they meet beside a stile one evening after she had left her present employment. At the agreed time she hurried to the stile, but her boyfriend was not there. Instead, she was surprised to find a hole dug, and a pick and spade lying close by. Seeing no one around, she climbed a nearby tree and waited. In due course her lover and another man came, and on reaching the stile and not seeing her there her boyfriend said, 'She will not come tonight. We will go home now and come back and kill her tomorrow night.'.

When they had gone, the girl quickly climbed down the tree and ran home. On meeting her father she poured out her whole story, and after a few minutes' thought he decided, 'We will have a feast and ask our friends, and we will ask thy sweetheart to come and also the man that came with him to the tree.'.

The evening of the feast arrived, and all the guests came including her lover and unknown friend. Late in the evening it was planned to play a game of riddles, and each of the guests stood up and recited a riddle for the others to unravel. The young girl was last, and she said:

'I'll rede you a riddle, I'll rede it you right,
Where was I last Saturday night?
The wind did blow, the leaves did shake,
When I saw the hole the fox did make.'

As soon as she had ended, her lover and friend hurriedly departed and were not seen again.

STOKE HALL

FAIR FLORA — THE GHOST OF STOKE HALL

Overlooking the village of Froggatt, the river Derwent and Froggatt Edge, is Stoke Hall, which was built in 1755. A maid-servant of the Hall, known as Flora, worked there about 120 years ago. She was deeply in love with a soldier who was fighting abroad. One night she was brutally murdered. The owners, who were deeply shocked at the deed, had a memorial erected to her in the front garden. A while later the owners happened to look out of the window at the memorial, and to their horror they saw it move. Most alarmed, they ordered the monument to be taken down and resited about half a mile away to the north.

In the 1970's the Hall has been converted into a hotel, and the owners at the time experienced strange and unanswerable phenomena which suggest the ghost of Fair Flora still haunts the Hall. On one occasion a workman had agreed to meet the owners to discuss the work to be done. While he waited in the kitchen, the bells suddenly rang. He searched the house and found no one. It was not until one hour later that the owners arrived. On another occasion the burglar alarm, which is triggered off by the disturbance of a beam of light rayss, suddenly rang. The building was searched and again no-one was found. When they returned to the monitor, the fault was still shown. Fifteen minutes later the fault cleared itself.

THE HARD DRIVING TAILOR

The following is a popular tale that was told in Calver in the late nineteenth century.

A tailor of the village was a noted slave-driver, and made his two apprentices work all day and most of the evening. Rarely did they leave their work before 11 p.m. After a few months of such treatment the apprentices were, naturally, rather fed up with this state of affairs. At last their opportunity came to get even. The previous night the tailor had told them that he would be away the following day to get more cloth and therefore would not be back until the evening. The following day his two apprentices worked away all day on the work that was assigned to them. In the early evening they left the shop and climbed a tree overlooking the path that the tailor would use on his return home. At last he came, and when he was close enough one of the apprentices called out, 'Abraham'. The tailor, who was a religious man, assumed that the Lord had summoned him, and he replied, 'Yes, my Lord.'. The voice from above continued: 'If thou keepest thy lads at work till eleven Thou shalt not enter the kingdom of heaven.'

Hearing this, the tailor continued on his way deep in thought, with a roll of cloth over his shoulder. The two apprentices quickly climbed down the tree and took a short cut back to their work. When the tailor arrived he found them hard at work. Without any preamble he said to them, 'Put your work away, lads, put your work away.'

Never from that day onwards did the apprentices work any later than 7.00 p.m. in the evening.

PRIESTLEY'S STONE

At the south-eastern end of Stanage Edge, near the Burbage Valley, is the Cowper Stone (marked on the Ordnance Survey map). Just below this stone is Priestley's Stone, sometimes known as Stump John. On it are engraved the initials I.P. These are believed to be the initials of John Priestley, who resided at Overstones Farm nearby. This farm was once a public house and the long curving road it is on is known as the Fiddler's Elbow, because of its shape.

During the grouse season, two beaters always came to this Stone and hid a bottle of ale near it. The bottle they had hidden the previous year was dug up and the contents drunk. In the words of the beaters, 'It wer' proper stingo!'.

THE VILLAGE PHILOSOPHER

In William Wood's book TALES AND TRADITIONS OF THE HIGH PEAK is the story of Old Gregory, who died in 1820. He lived in the Peak District, but precisely where I cannot discover. He was an avid reader and had a remarkable thirst for knowledge on any subject. At the age of twenty, 'in history, science, and poetry, he revelled at large, grasping also with the energy of a heaven-gifted intellect, the endless and airy subtleties of metaphysical science'. He was also extremely well versed in astrology and was looked upon with considerable awe. The locals said he could 'rule planets, cast nativities and predict events'.

Old Gregory lived the life of a hermit, preoccupied with his search for all forms of knowledge. If he ventured out, it was most often to one of the nearby large houses where he might spend hours in the library devouring each and every book of literature. He would be seen walking along the road in his old grey suit, which was secured at the waist by a flaxen cord. Late in life, when his span was nearly complete, he was visited by the rector who came to give him a new suit. His last one he had worn for twenty years. But he refused the gift, saying 'No, I feel the finger of death, and my sinking frame shall not be garnished at last by the vestments of charity and the offerings of pride.'

A few weeks later he was close to death and he lay upon a wooden settie to die. A friend who was with him suggested that it would be better if he had his head raised, and Old Gregory remarked, 'Bring a sod or stone for that purpose; soon will my mortal body be a handful of dust.'

He died later that day.

A LADY'S TALE

I have found several stories about one elderly who lived in either the Hope or Curbar area in the late nineteenth century. Whenever her grandchildren came she would sit them on her knee and tell them about the world. The actual edge of the world, in her account, was the limestone pinnacles of Dovedale. Beyond that was 'the bad place', the phrase she used for hell. Like all elderly ladies of this time she sat in a rocking chair and smoked a long clay pipe.

She was a very superstitious lady, and any untoward incident she took as a warning of some kind. There were two such incidents that she was very fond of recalling. One was when a sheep dog howled at night and she recognised that as news that the farmer had died. The other was when a white cricket crossed the hearth. She later learnt that on that night a girl lost her way in a snowstorm and was frozen to death.

COCKEY FARM

Cockey Farm is situated just south of Abney village, at Grid Reference SK199794. It is said to have been named after two cock-eyed men who met there. One said, 'Ah wish thou'd look wheear thour't gooin', and the other replied, 'Ah wish thou'd go wheear thour't lookin'.

Another version states that the farm was named after an owner who was cock-eyed.

Born in the farm in 1750 was William Newton. His father was a joiner, and when William was old enough he went into his father's trade. He proved a very skilful carpenter and worked in many of the houses in this area of Derbyshire. It was through working in these larger houses that he was introduced to the world of books. This interest in the written word proved a lifelong pursuit, and later, encouraged by the Reverend Cunningham, Curate of Eyam, he wrote poetry. He was also spurred on in this activity by Anna Seward, the Lichfield poetess. As a result many of his poems appeared in the Gentleman's Magazine.

In 1780 he was appointed the head carpenter for the Duke of Devonshire's building, the Crescent at Buxton. This building, one of the masterpieces of Derbyshire, has 380 windows, and a sweeping curved facade of 200 feet length with wings extending a further 58 feet on either side. It is reputed to have cost £120,000 to build, and the money is said to have come from the profits of the Duke's Ecton copper mine in the Manifold valley. The designer of the Crescent was John Carr of York. William went on to be head carpenter of Cressbrook Mill. Later, when it burnt down, he and three others built a new one. Eventually he owned this mill and employed about two hundred children here, becoming well-known for his sensitive and humane treatment of his charges. It was from his poetry that he earned himself a place in Derbyshire history. He became nicknamed the 'Minstrel of the Peak'. He died in 1830, and in the churchyard of Tideswell church can be seen his tomb, which bears his title — 'Minstrel of the Peak'.

GOTHERAGE BARN

MURDER IN GOTHERAGE BARN

Down in the quiet secluded Bretton Clough, just north of Bretton, a murder is believed to have taken place in Gotherage Barn (Grid Reference SK213793) in about 1780. The barn was once a seventeenth century farmhouse. There are two versions of the murder.

One states that a man named Blinker Bland who lived at Abney came to the farm. Here he struck the farmer over the head with a milk stool and killed him. His wife escaped and raced to the nearest dwelling just over a quarter of a mile away, Bretton Clough Farm . She was terrified, and ran clad only in her nightdress, shouting continually, 'Nah Blinker, it's thee'.

The other version states that several masked men entered the farm. The farmer recognised one of them and said, 'Blinker, Blinker, ah know thee!'. The masked men took little heed and searched the house for money, but found none. The farmer had only recently put £400 into the bank. The men were furious at not finding any money, and in their rage murdered both the farmer and his wife. Their child hid, and when the men had gone he ran to Bretton Clough Farm and told them what had happened. Whether justice was ever done, I regret to say I do not know.

BRETTON'S RACE COURSE

The sheep races at Bretton are known to have taken place up to about 1835, and were most probably held in early August. As far as I know, they were unique in Derbyshire.

The wildest ram was found from the neighbourhood and covered with soap, to make handling almost impossible. The idea was to catch the ram along the race course. The race course was about half a mile long, and ran from the Barrel Inn to an old barn on the northern slopes of Sir William Hill.

A MOCK MARRIAGE

In J. Pendleton's HISTORY OF DERBYSHIRE is the following:-

'A stone in the corner of the vestry records the death of Joseph Hunt, rector of Eyam, who was buried December 16th, 1709, and of his wife Ann, who died six years previously. She was the daughter of a village publican, whom he had been obliged by the Bishop to marry in consequence of his having gone through a mock ceremony with her in a drunken freak. This caused an action of breach of promise with a Derby lass to whom he was previously engaged. Some years passed in litigation, which drained his purse and estranged his friends; and eventually he had to take shelter in the vestry (which some say was built for that purpose) where he resided the remainder of his life to keep the law hounds at bay.'

Joseph Hunt became rector of Eyam on March 21, 1684. Not long afterwards he was asked to baptise the child of Matthew Ferns, who was the landlord of the Miners' Arms in Eyam. After the ceremony the young rector stayed and joined in with the merrymaking and drinking. He became far from sober, and began making eyes at the landlord's daughter Anne, who was aged eighteen. Shortly afterwards the celebrations got out of hand, and, in front of everyone, he performed a mock marriage ceremony with Anne, using a Common Prayer book. News of this night's revelry soon spread, and it was not long before the Bishop of Derby learned what had happened. The Bishop insisted that he marry Anne as soon as possible. However, this was a little difficult as Joseph was already engaged to another. He managed to extract himself from this engagement, although law suits followed for the rest of his life. He married Anne on September 4, 1684. Details of the whole story can be seen in the Miners' Arms at Eyam.

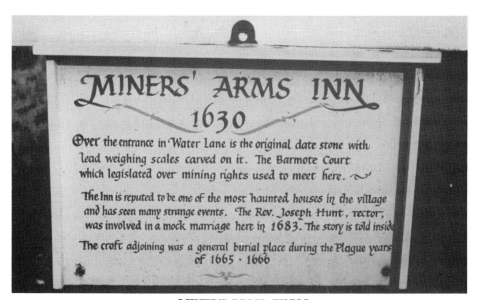

MINER'S ARMS, EYAM

45

THE GHOST OF EYAM DELL

In the late eighteenth and early nineteenth centuries a female ghost was frequently seen on the outskirts of Eyam, in the quiet sheltered dale between Eyam and Stoney Middleton. People who saw her recorded that she was middle-aged, wore a bed gown, a mob-cap on her head and that her shoes always had shiny buckles. She was frequently seen crossing the dale at a furious speed, and other times late at night she would 'strip the bedclothes off the bed while the trembling occupants were almost paralysed with frozen fear'. The occupants lived in a cottage in the dale. As time passed everyone ensured that they never walked up the dale in the dark.

One of the regulars to the nearby Ball Inn in the early nineteenth century was Tom Cockeye, a leadminer. He was well liked, a widower and a person who always told a good joke. On one occasion he became far from sober and submitted to the tauntings of the other drinkers and the landlord's French wife, Blandy. Everyone knew that his way home lay up the quiet dale.

'Cheer up! Cheer up! Cockeye', said Blandy, 'not afraid of a woman nor her spirit certain!'

'Not the Devil either, with another quart, eh! lads!', replied Cockeye.

'Come, come, this is too grave a subject to be lightly talked about', said the landlord.

'Tis said, mon cher, that the woman whose spirit still wanders the dell came to an untimely end, or death', said Blandy.

'Another drop, good landlady, and I'll ask her that question this night', said Cockeye, who was now quite drunk.

About 3 a.m. everyone parted and began walking their separate ways home. Tom walked up the dale, and the higher he came the more misgivings he had. To be blunt he was petrified. As he approached the cottage he saw the ghost. She came speedily towards him, and with her icy fingers firmly gripped about him Tom was dragged down the dale. By this time he had lost consciousness. Next morning he was awakened by the landlord of the Ball Inn. It is said that from that moment onwards Tom Cockeye never touched a drop of alcohol and remained a sober man for the rest of his life.

A BODY IN CARLSWARK CAVERN

In the eighteenth century there were many more festivals, market days, wakes or fairs held in the Peak District than there are today. Pedlars made a living from moving from one fair to another, selling trinkets. A Scotsman always toured the area every summer, and came as usual to the Eyam Wakes in late August. Shortly after he arrived he noticed several other pedlars whom he had never seen before. He soon learned from speaking to them that they did not possess the necessary permit. Sensing he was losing trade to these illegal vendors, he had a quiet word with the local policeman.

Acting as though he was unaware of the other pedlars' guilt, the policeman asked to see their permits. As they were unable to show them he told the pedlars to stop selling and pack up to go. Annoyed at their betrayal, the pedlars left, and as they passed the Scotsman told him that they would get even with him.

Later in the day the Scotsman had to go to Stoney Middleton, and mentioned his journey to the landlord of the Bull's Head. Whereupon he told the Scotsman that the other pedlars were after his blood. To be on the safe side, he would ask his barman to accompany him to Stoney Middleton. The two of them set off together, and arrived at the village about half an hour later. The Scotsman parted from the barman and went about his business. On passing the Moon Inn, he met the other pedlars. Although he did not want anything to do with them, they appeared friendly and wanted to forget about their poaching. Upon the suggestion that he should join them in a game of cards, he consented.

Around a table the six pedlars sat and, between glasses of ale, played cards. The game was a merry one, with much laughing. However, this facade did not last long. Waiting their opportunity, they picked an argument with the Scotsman. With the barman looking on, they murdered him.

The five pedlars continued to sit round the table, acting normally, until everyone had gone. When the street was quiet, the Scotsman's body was taken on horseback to Carlswark Cavern. Two of them carried the body inside and dumped it several hundred yards from the entrance. A couple of drunken miners witnessed this moonlit funeral procession, but their story was so incoherent that it was never believed.

No questions were asked, and the five were never brought to trial. Justice is believed to have been served, for the five, who came from Tideswell, suffered from guilt to such an extent that they were always miserable. The female member of the group suffered facial disfiguration, as a result of cancer. The landlord of the Moon Inn, although his lips remained sealed for fear of being murdered himself, underwent trying times. On his death bed he had to be moved from the Inn to a neighbour's house before his troubled mind would allow him to die!

There the tale would have ended, had it not been for the discovery of the Scotsman's body, twenty years later. 'Even when crime is thought to be securely buried, it will, in time, roll out of its grave.' (Aries — Young England) How true this quotation is!

Nearing the Eyam Wakes, a young couple, named Betty and Peter, were busy preparing their cottage for some guests who were coming to stay. On the first morning of the wakes, Betty arose early while Peter, who had had a restless night, slept on. When Peter finally climbed out of bed, he met Betty downstairs.

'Bless me', said Betty, 'What a sorrowful look you've got on for a feast day in the morning; I thought you would have been all joy, like a lark at its martins.'

'Ah! Betty, I hope I do not experience the sorrow I feel', Peter replied.

'Sorrow! Sorrow?' said the wondering wife.

'Hearken, I dreamed our friends and I were walking in Middleton Dale.'

Peter dreamed that he and his guests went for a walk. On reaching Carlswark Cavern, one of the guests suggested they go inside and have a look. Everyone being keen at the suggestion, Peter took them in. While creeping along a narrow passage, Peter came across a body. Letting out a startled cry of terror, everyone turned round and quickly retreated. Apart from the horror, what troubled him most was the thought that somehow he knew the dead person well. Before they could discuss it any further, the guests began to arrive and the dream was forgotten about.

Following a satisfying meal the female guests and Betty sat down to gossip. The men and Peter went for a stroll around the village. Having seen the various places of interest, such as the Cross, Katherine Mompesson's tomb and the cottage where the first plague victim died, they descended the road towards Stoney Middleton. On nearing Carlswark Cavern, someone proposed, for a bit of fun, to explore the Cavern. With everyone keen to have a look, Peter could hardly refuse. Armed with several candles which they fetched from a nearby house, they entered the cavern.

The entrance was originally large, similar to but smaller than Peak Cavern at Castleton. The villagers of Stoney Middleton used the entrance as a place to store their wagons, and during the summer months it was also a favourite sleeping place for tramps. Peter led them into the passageways, almost terrified to walk, for fear of finding a body. After a few minutes he relaxed and began enjoying this excursion into the bowels of the earth. Probing ahead with his candle, suddenly the flickering flame picked out the shape of a skeleton. His heart jumped. He stared yet again, unbelieving, before shrieking aloud, dropping his candle, turning and running with others to the entrance.

Peter reported his findings to the police, but it was next day before they came to remove the body and clothes. Meanwhile news of the discovery spread like a whirlwind, and a large crowd had assembled to watch the policemen.

'For now the Scotsman issued from the cave,
of Carlswark dark, his sepulchre and grave.'

(Richard Furness — THE PARNASSUS OF THE PEAK)

The only identifiable piece of material was the buckles on the shoes. Being original and unusual, people were able to say with certainty that they were the Scotsman's. The body was placed in a box and kept for many years in a corner of the north aisle of Eyam Church. One of the 'dares' of the village was to have a peep inside! Since no relative came forward, the body and clothes were buried in the churchyard. The shoes were still in good condition, and shortly before burial the bell ringer, Matthew Hall, took them. He wore them for some time until they collapsed.

THE MOON INN

After the discovery no one ventured again into the passageways for many years. Those who did go near often remarked about a ghost they had seen of the Scotsman. Horses always shied away, if they came close to the cavern. Being an unsavoury place, the local authority began using the entrance as a refuse tip. This is the reason why, until recently, only a small passageway was left. This passage has now been opened out by potholers who wanted to explore the cave system. With 4,000 feet of passageways, today it is a popular cavern amongst speleologists. Fortunately, they do not have to contend with skeletons, but simply overcome a fear of dark places!

TIDESWELL

49

THE DRUNKEN BUTCHER OF TIDESWELL

William Bennet, who lived in Tideswell during the late eighteenth century, was, apart from owning a weaving factory, a poet. His ballads, such as 'The Cavalier', 'The King of the Peak' and the 'Drunken Butcher of Tideswell', were extremely popular. The last ballad is the story of a butcher who, following a drunken party at Sparrowpit, was chased over the moors by a ghost, as he rode home to Tideswell. The following are a few of the verses.

Oh, list to me, ye yeomen all,
Who live in dale or down!
My song is of a butcher tall,
Who lived in Tiddeswell town.
In bluff King Harry's merry days,
He slew both sheep and kine;
And drank his fill of nut brown ale,
In lack of good red wine.

Now draw thy rein, thou jolly Butcher;
How far hast thou to ride?
To Waylee-Bridge, to Simon the Tanner,
To sell this good cow-hide.
Thou shalt not go one foot ayont,
till thou light and sup with me;
And when thou'st emptied my measure of liquor,
I'll have a measure wi' thee.

Oh no, oh no, thou jolly parson!
I cannot tarry, I say;
I was drunk last night, and if I tarry,
I'se be drunk again today.
What likes, what likes, cried the Pardoner then,
Why tellest thou that to me?
Thou may'st e'en get thee drunk this blessed night;
And well shrived for both thou shalt be.

Then down got the Butcher from his horse,
I wot full fain was he;
And he drank 'till the summer sun went down,
And the stars began to shine;
And his greasy noddle, was dazed and addle,
With the nut brown ale and wine.

Bold Robin the Butcher was horsed and away;
And a drunken wight was he;
For sometimes his blood-red eyes saw double;
And then he could scantly see.
The forest trees seemed to stately dance,
As he rode so swift along;
And the forest trees, to his wildered sense,
Resang the jovial song.

Just then the moon, from behind the rack,
Burst out into open view;
And on the sward and purple heath
Broad light and shadow threw;
And there the Butcher, whose heart beat quick,
With fear of Gramarye,
Fast by his side, as he did ride,
A foul phantom did espy.

But ever as fast as the Butcher rode,
The Ghost did grimly glide:
Now down on the earth before his horse,
Then fast his rein beside.
O'er stock and rock, and stone and pit,
O'er hill and dale and down,
'Till Robin the Butcher gained his door-stone,
In Tiddeswell's good old town.

Oh, what thee ails, thou drunken Butcher?
Said his wife, as he sank down;
And what thee ails, thou drunken Butcher?
Cried one-half of the Town.
I have seen a Ghost, it hath raced my horse,
For three good miles and more;
And it vanished within the Churchyard wall,
As I sank down at the door.

Beshrew thy heart, for a drunken beast!
Cried his wife, as she held him there;
Beshrew thy heart, for a drunken beast,
And a coward, with heart of hare.
No Ghost hath raced thy horse to-night;
Nor evened his wit with thine:
The Ghost was thy shadow, thou drunken wretch!
I would the Ghost were mine.

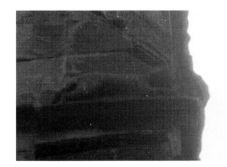

TIDESWELL CHURCH CAT

Tideswell Church is famed all over England as a prime example of fourteenth century ecclesiastic building. To Derbyshire people, it is affectionately known as the 'Cathedral of the Peak'. High on the north side of the tower, which was the last part of the church to be built, on the very corner of the moulding, to the right of the window, is a carved cat. It is said that when the workmen were working on the tower at this height a cat climbed up to them. To record the occasion the workmen carved a walking cat on the moulding.

THE RULES OF THE BELLRINGERS OF TIDESWELL (About 1770)

All gentlemen that intend to ring
See that these laws you keep in everything:-
When first that you into the belfry come
See that the ringers have convenient room;
For if you be an hindrance unto them,
Fourpence you forfeit to these gentlemen.
For every oath you swear ere you go hence,
You must immediately pay just sixpence.
For every bell turn'd o'er, without delay
Fourpence you must unto the present clerk pay;
And if that you're desirous for to ring,
With hat or spurs on do not touch one string;
For if you do your forfeit is for that
Fourpence pay down or else you lose your hat.
And if you have a mind to be enrolled
A ringer here, these orders you must hold.

This is similar to Hathersage's notice and makes an interesting comparison.

TIDESWELL TALES

The following Tideswell Tales bear a strong resemblance to the renowned Gotham Tales of Nottinghamshire. At Gotham King John came to the village and was met by the villagers, who told him that the route he took through their village would from henceforward be a public road. King John was annoyed at such a confrontation, and on reaching Nottingham he sent a select group to Gotham to learn more about these people, with the intention of bringing them to trial. The Gotham people knew they had aroused the wrath of the King and so, when his envoy arrived, they all did strange things, to give the envoy the idea that they were all fools. This did the trick, and the King's men returned to Nottingham to report their findings. The King laughed at their antics, and the whole episode was forgotten as he assumed the village was full of fools.

How the Tideswell Tales evolved I cannot find out, but these are some of the odd and foolish things the 'Tideswell Fool' did. It should be borne in mind that Tideswell is called 'Tidser'.

1. A Tidser man lay down on the ground to paint the underneath of his barrow. When it was dry, instead of wheeling it to the owner, some three miles away, he carried it on his back.

2. A Tidserite wanted to dry his tallow candles, so placed them in a hot oven.

3. A cuckoo was calling in a nearby field, so several
Tidserites built a stone wall around the cuckoo to keep
it in.

4. One Tidserite went into a field with his rod and line and
fished for the moon.

5. Before putting his horse in the field to graze, the
Tidserite fitted a nosebag onto the horse.

6. On Whit Monday, when the Friendly Society was holding its
annual club walk, a female of the village lifted her pig
onto the wall so that it could clearly see the activities.

7. A group of farmers who had been selling hay were returning
to Tideswell in the dark. On their journey they lost
their way, and on reaching a signpost they lifted up a
young boy who, with matches, was supposed to read what
the sign said. He lit several matches but could not read,
and finally said to his father, 'Aw conna reyd it feyther;
t' letters is too big.'.

A TALE FROM TIDESWELL

Living in Tideswell in the nineteenth century was an amusing character called 'Owd Whacky'.
One day he had the chance of buying a very old cheese. Without any hesitation he purchased
it. When he returned home with the cheese he found he could not cut or break off a single
piece, for it was so old and rock hard. He was so determined to cut it open that eventually he
decided to climb the church tower and throw it to the ground, where he hoped it would smash
into pieces. While he was climbing to the top, an elderly couple were sitting in their house
near the church and were busy praying for food. Owd Whacky threw the cheese from the top,
and instead of breaking on impact with the ground the cheese simply bounced from a
gravestone, rolled across the road and leapt into the house of the elderly couple. The man
turned to his wife and said full of emotion,

'Ah, wench; tha' sees th' Lord's sent us a cheyse.'

TIDESWELL CHURCH — TOWER

WHESTON HALL

THE GHOST OF WHESTON HALL

A mile and a half west of Tideswell is the quiet and secluded village of Wheston. The Hall, which dates back to the seventeenth century, is the setting for several ghost stories, and this is but one.

Once a year a female ghost, clad only in her nightgown, walks barefoot three times round the Hall. As she walks she pulls at her golden hair and shrieks aloud. The woman is said to have married a man she did not wish to. The man whom she loved and wanted to marry, on learning of her marriage to another, moved to Wheston Hall to live a life of solitude. He rarely saw anyone, and the villagers began to make fanciful stories about him. They said his only visitor was the Devil, who came with his long tail and cloven feet. In due course the lady left her husband and came to her lover at the Hall and there she stayed. Alas, her husband found her, murdered her lover and left, never to be seen again. She continued to live at the Hall, heartbroken, until she died and was buried in Tideswell. As penance for her broken loves she returns once a year to the Hall.

CHELMORTON CHURCH

'OWD ALICK' — A CHELMORTON CHARACTER

Alexander Ollerenshaw was born on September 1, 1753, and lived in Chelmorton all his life. Chelmorton, which has the highest parish church in England, lies six miles south-east of Buxton. 'Owd Alick' became the village blacksmith and the landlord of the Blacksmith's Arms.

Not long afterwards he immersed himself in the idea of perpetual motion.

> 'He got it into his head that he would be the discoverer of the Perpetual Motion, and so deeply was this idea fixed in his mind that he sacrificed the most valuable portion of his time and energy in pursuing that end which he believed he was destined to accomplish.'

Every day for many years he would slip into a back room of the inn and work away at his machine. If anyone had misgivings about his project, Owd Alick used a strange argument for his confidence of success. He said, 'Yo, 'appen dunna know, what Sir Isaac Newton said. Hey said, as th' perpetual motion o'd bi fun aht, and th' discovery o'd bi made by an idiot.'

Although he lived to be 88 years of age the project was never completed and was later broken up and kept by various people in remembrance of him. He died on October 16, 1841. Over thirty years after his death, his memory still lingered in the village.

> 'Poor owd chap! He troid hard bur hey cudna dow't. He wor a good feller nobody's enemy bur his own. Iv'ry boddy loik'd owd Alick.'

WORMHILL HALL

'OWD NICK' OF WORMHILL

Nicholas Bower, who was better known as Owd Nick or just plain Nick, was a shepherd for Mr. Bagshaw of Wormhill Hall. Although a rather dim and scatter-brained person, he was an extremely competent shepherd and was never known to lose a single sheep. He was a humorous person, full of quaint sayings and dry humour, and therefore was popular at the Hall. A story is told about him that he was once invited to the Hall for the evening when Mr. Bagshaw had a guest staying, who had an exceptionally long nose. Owd Nick came for the evening and remained silent, which was most unusual for him. Eventually Mr. Bagshaw asked what was the matter, and Nick replied, 'Well, I remember yer honour towd me this mornin' not to speak th' gentleman's big nose!' Everyone thought this was immensely funny, even the gentleman concerned, who showed he was not at all offended by giving Nick a shilling (5p).

A little later Nick left the room, and once outside he wrapped the shilling in a piece of paper and hid it in a wall. He was watched doing this, although he was unaware of this. He walked away, and a little while later he returned and removed his shilling. He unwrapped the paper and was surprised to find that he now had two. Thinking he was onto a good thing, he quickly wrapped the shillings up again and hid them once more in the wall. He came back several minutes later and found he now had 2s.6d.(12.5p). Seeing that he was not making as much money as on his last visit he pocketed the money and said, 'It's growin', it's growin', it's growin' varra fast; but it may ha' a blight on't, so I'll een purrit i' my poke while it's a'reet!'

PARSON'S TOR, LATHKILL DALE

PARSON'S TOR

In that beautiful limestone valley, Lathkill Dale, opposite the cave where the river enters the dale floor, is Parson's Tor. Originally it was known as Fox's Tor, but this is the tale as to how it became known as Parson's Tor. On October 11, 1776, the vicar of Monyash, the Reverend Robert Lomas, set off for Bakewell to see the vicar there. The weather was bad and he left late at night, after a good meal and wine, to return home.

> 'Ah! thick was the mist on the moor that night,
> Poor wight, he had lost his way!
> The north-west wind blowing strong on his right,
> To the left had made him stray.'

In fact he was totally lost and unable to see a yard in front of him. Unknowingly he reached the top of Fox Tor, and here the horse would go no further. Finally the horse was so frightened that he suddenly bolted. As for the vicar -

> 'Then headlong fell he o'er the lofty cliff,
> He shrieked, and sank in the gloom;
> Down — down to the bottom he swiftly sped,
> And death was his dreadful doom.
>
> The dead man lay cold on the blood-stained rocks -
> The darkness did him enshroud;
> And the owls high up in the ivy-clad tor,
> Bewailed him all night full loud.'

The next morning the people of Monyash assumed the vicar had stayed in Bakewell because of the weather, but -

'Bad tidings from Bakewell — no Parson there -
No Parson could else be found;
'Twas noon, yet no tidings — they still searched on,
And missed they no likely ground.

At last the searchers went into the dale.
And there at the foot of Fox Tor -
They found the Parson, all cold and dead,
'Mong the rocks all stained with gore.'

He was found dead on October 12, 1776, and for a long while the village kept a tuft of grass which the vicar held in his hand in a glass bottle.

'You may not now see in Monyash town
The deadman's sear tuft of grass;
But still it is there, in memory stored,
And thence it shall never pass.

You may not now find Fox Tor by that name,
The swain thus knows it no more;
But pointing thereat from the Lathkil grot,
He'll shew you the Parson's Tor.'

The extracts above were taken from the poem THE PARSON'S TOR by the Reverend W.R. Bell, formerly curate of Bakewell. It was first published in the RELIQUARY in 1864.

JACK MIDGE — THE POACHER

Poaching was one of the many pastimes in Derbyshire, with the large grouse shooting estates in its northern half. One of the most famous Derbyshire poachers was John Marshall, who was better known as Jack Midge. The Derbyshire Times on Friday, September 17, 1886, recorded that Jack had made his 29th appearance in Court for poaching. He had been 'working' on land belonging to Major McCreagh-Thornhill of Gratton, near Elton. The gamekeeper had caught him redhanded as he was busy trying to snare rabbits.

He was fined 40 shillings (£2) plus costs or, if he could not pay, a month's hard labour. He paid, for 'a poacher pays his captors out of their own pockets'. If he had been caught on someone's land, he always made a special note to go there again and recoup his losses! Later Midge became a paid gamekeeper for Major McCreagh-Thornhill.

SINGING SAM OF DERBYSHIRE

Wandering around the Peak District in the mid-eighteenth century was this odd character, Sam, who earned his livelihood from singing ballads. A portrait of him by Williams, dated 1760, shows him to be small in size. His face was pointed, with small eyes and snub nose. On his thick curly hair he wore a large saucer-shaped hat. The portrait depicts him in a thigh-long coat belted at the waist, knee breeches, of which his right one is ripped at the knee, and with his shoes unlaced. To accompany his songs, which he composed himself, he used a 'blether fiddle', or bladder fiddle, which was quite common in the Peak District at his time.

'His instrument was as quaint and curious as himself. It consisted of a straight staff nearly as tall as himself, with a single string tied fast around it at each end. This he tightened with a fully inflated cow's bladder, which assisted very materially the tone of the rude instrument. His bow was a rough stick of hazel or briar, with a single string; and with this, with the lower end of his staff nesting on the ground, and the upper grasped by his right hand, which he passed up and down to tighten or slacken the string as he played, he scraped away and produced sounds which, though not so musical as those of Paganini and his single string, would no doubt harmonise with Sam's rude ballad and ruder voice.'

His most popular ballad, which he is said to have composed, is 'The Beggar's Ramble'. There are four known versions of the ballad, and here are extracts from just one of them, which is twenty-five verses long.

Opening verse -

Hark ye well, my neighbours all, and pray now can you tell
Which is the nearest way unto the Beggar's well?
There is Eaton, and Toten, and Brancot on the hill,
There's Beggarly Beeston, and lousy Chilwell.

There's Wingfield, and Tupton, from there to the Claycross,
From there I went to Chesterfield — was almost cut to loss,
There's Asher, and there's Firbeck, and Stretton on the hill,
There's Hickam, and Oakerthorpe, and so for Wiremill.

There's Hollongton and Middleton-by-Youlgreave I've heard tell,
There's Bonsall and there's Winster, from and to Bakewell,
There's Wardlemire and Uckler, from there to Hoyland came,
And when I did thither get, I began to feel quite lame.

There's Darley by Derby, for that is a shady bower,
And Derby is a country town; there's handsome Micklover.
There's Littleover, and Mackworth, and so for Etwall I went,
Until at last I did arrive at Burton-upon-Trent.

Last verse

There's Stapleford, and Risley, and Draycott also,
At last I came to Breaston, where I wish'd for long ago,
So I hope these lines which I have wrote no one they will
offend,
For at every door there stands a whore, at Leek Town end.

ASHFORD — HYDE PLAQUE

BRIDGE LEAPS

At Ashford-in-the-Water, on the second bridge over the river Wye, (Grid Reference SK199696, opposite the cricket field and now a No Through Road.) is the inscription — 'M. HYDE, 1664'. According to the tale a man who had been at the mill in Taddington was riding his horse astride a bag of meal. As he crossed the bridge a sudden gust of wind blew him off the horse, over the parapet and into the water. Here he drowned.

On the eastern side of Cromford (Grid Reference SK300573) on the bridge over the Derwent a stone had the following inscription — 'The Leap of R.M. B.H. Mare, June, 1697'.

CROMFORD — B.H.MARE PLAQUE

MONSAL DALE

THE WIZARD OF MONSAL DALE

Living in a limestone cave in Monsal Dale during the 1820s was Neddy Higgins and his daughter Betty. In the surrounding area they were renowned for their skills of magic. Neddy was regarded as a wizard and his daughter a witch, and both were capable of casting and removing spells. They were also able to predict events and solve mysterious disappearances, and other knotty problems. Neddy does not appear to have done any work. Instead, Betty begged and went round collecting rags and bones.

One day his farmer had lost his sheep and went to Neddy to see if he could, through his powers, locate the flock. Before the farmer went to Neddy, he knew for certain that Neddy had stayed in the cave for days previously and would not have known about the disappearance of his sheep. Neddy listened to the details before resting his head in his hands and going into deep thought. After a few minutes he drew some lines on the floor with a stick and said,

'Up by Tideswell and round by the moor
John, at the gate, has dug up a floor.'

After this utterance he added nothing else, leaving the farmer to solve the riddle. Shortly afterwards the meaning came clear, for a man named John had indeed taken up some floor boards and hidden the sheep. Sheep stealing in these days was a very serious offence and often ended in the thief being hanged. This case was no exception.

BAKEWELL PUDDING

In about 1859 the cook at the Rutland Arms Hotel in Bakewell misunderstood her instructions and made a pudding instead of a tart. The mistress of the hotel was Mrs. Greaves, who was the sister-in-law of Sir Joseph Paxton. She told her cook to put the mixture onto the pastry case and then spread jam on top. Instead the cook did it the other way round, putting the jam in first followed by the mixture. The result was liked by all and has since become a well-known delicacy. Mrs. Greaves, in her will, left the recipe to a Mr. Radford. This later passed to a Mr. Bloomer, and descendants still make the puddings to the original recipe.

BAKEWELL TOMB EPITAPHS

The tomb which bears the following epitaph is just on the left-hand side of the main entrance to the church.

'Know posterity that on the 8th of April in the year
of grace 1757 the rambling remains of the abovesaid
John Dale were in the 88th year of his pilgrimage
laid upon his two wives. This thing in life might
raise some jealousie: Here all three lye together
lovingly, but from embraces here no pleasure flows,
alike are here all human joys and woes. Here Sarah's
chiding John no longer hears and old John's rambling
Sarah no more fears, a period's come to all their
toilsome lives, the goodman's quiet, still are both
his wives.'

BAKEWELL CHURCH

Inside the church to the left of the north door is the following epitaph.

'To the memory of
Matthew Strutt of this town farrier;
Long fam'd in these parts for his
veterinary skill;
A good neighbour, and
A staunch friend to church and king.
Being church warden, at the time
The present peal of eight bells were hung,
Thro' his zeal for the house of God, and
unremitting attention
To the airy business of the belfry
he caught a cold which
terminated his existence May 25th, 1798;
in the 68th year of his age.'

ANOTHER TOMB IN BAKEWELL CHURCHYARD reads -

'Erected in remembrance of PHILLIP ROE
who died 12th September, 1815 aged 52 years.
The vocal powr's here let us mark
of Phillip our late Parish Clerk
In church none ever heard a layman
With a clearer voice say Amen
Who now with Hallelujahs sound
Like him can make the roof rebound
The choir lament his choral tones
The town — so soon here lie his bones
Sleep undisturbed within
Thy peaceful shrine
Till angels wake thee
With such notes as thine.'

ROCHE ABBEY

ONE ASH GRANGE

If a building is called a Grange, it signifies some connection with an abbey. One Ash Grange, one mile south east of Monyash, was connected with the Cistercian Abbey — Roche Abbey, near Maltby in South Yorkshire. Monks who misbehaved at the Abbey were sent to One Ash Grange as penance. The building is now a farm, and still growing there is a unique species of rhubarb which is known as 'the monks' rhubarb' as they are reputed to have planted it originally. Close to the house is a small cave in the limestone which is known as 'the monks' cell', but it has yet to be proved that it was used for this purpose. Mrs. Gaskell, the well-known nineteenth century novelist, wrote a novel set around the grange.

ANN MOORE

TWO FASTING DAMSELS

In 1761 Anne Moore was born near Ashbourne. At the age of 27 she married, but the marriage did not last long, and she became a servant. In 1807 she was living in Tutbury, which is just outside the Derbyshire boundary in Staffordshire. At about this time she learnt of Martha Taylor's fast (16 months without food in 1668) and saw it as an easy way to earn money, and so pretended to fast. After completing thirteen days without food, an account was published which brought people to see this 'remarkable woman'. She would be watched for nine days without a break before Anne asked all to leave to let her daughter see her. Her daughter would come in and secretly give her food. At first this secret eating was not noticed, and all the people who visited her gave her money which eventually accumulated to £250.

However, as time passed, people began to doubt her and in April 1813 a committee was formed to keep a close watch on her to ascertain whether her fast was genuine or not. The committee decided that she must fast for a month. Anne was naturally reluctant but had no option but to do so. After nine days she was on the verge of dying and her deception was revealed. She was made to sign the following confession on May 4, 1813.

'I, Anne Moore of Tutbury, humbly asking pardon of all persons whom I have attempted to deceive and impose upon, and above all, with unfeigned sorrow and contrition
imploring the divine mercy and forgiveness of that God whom
I have greatly offended, do most solemnly declare that I
have occasionally taken sustenance for the last six years.'

Of what became of her after this, little is known. In February 1816 she went to Prison, 'for falsely collecting money under the pretence of charity'.

In the Chapel-en-le-Frith register is the following entry:-

'On March 16th 1716, one Phoenix, a girl about 13 years of
age, a parish apprentice with W. Ward of Peak Forest, went
from George Bowden's house, of Lane End, about five o'clock
in the morning, towards her master's house. She sat down
at Peaslow (a mile east of Chapel-en-le-Frith) between the
ruts of G. Bowden's part (or road) that day and the next,
and the Friday, Saturday and Sunday following, two of which
days — viz. the 16th and 17th — were the most severe for
snowing and driving rain that hath been seen in the memory
of man. She was found alive on Monday, about one o'clock,
by W. Jackson of Sparrowpit and W. Longden of Peak Forest,
and after a slender refreshment of a little hot milk, was
carried to her master's house, and is now (March 25th 1717)
very well with only a little stiffness in her limbs. This
was the Lord's doing, and will be marvelled in future
generations. She ate no meat during the six days, nor was
she hungry, but very thirsty, and slept much.'

PRINCE ARTHUR

Prince Arthur, the Prince of Wales, was the eldest son and heir apparent of Henry the Seventh – 1485-1509. His Governor and Treasurer was Sir Henry Vernon, whose principal home was Haddon Hall near Bakewell. The prince was a frequent visitor to Haddon. When he was twelve years of age he had been betrothed to marry Catherine, the fourth daughter of Ferdinand, King of Castile and Aragon. The marriage had been performed by proxy at the chapel of Bewdley Manor. Sir Henry Vernon was one of the witnesses to the contract.

The prince enjoyed staying at Haddon and often explored the neighbourhood. In September 1501, he sat beside the Great Cross close to the cross roads, just over a mile south of Hassop. The Cross is now beside Bakewell church. While he rested he dozed off to sleep and dreamt that a woman dressed in white appeared before him and said,

> 'Unhappy, royal Prince, mourn not that fate which is not
> thine! One earthy pageant awaits thee, yea, it is at
> hand; and then, ah! then thou wilt drop into the lap of
> thy mother — ah, thy mother earth! Forth comes to
> Britain's shore thy lovely, smiling bride — ah! bride and
> widow of a royal boy!'

He awoke startled but saw no one. The dream foretold his future accurately, although he did not know it at the time. He returned to Haddon and was met by Sir Henry and many others who informed him that his wife had arrived from Spain. They were married soon afterwards and Prince Arthur died after being married only four months. His last words were, 'O, the vision of the cross at Haddon!'

HADDON HALL

66

A TALE OF HADDON HALL

In the early sixteenth century John Taylor, a butcher from Darley Dale, provided the Hall with meat, bringing it on a Friday. For the two months prior to Christmas, the two butlers had noticed the disappearance of two pounds of butter every time John Taylor came. Each Friday the butter was placed on a table in the banqueting hall for inspection by the lady of the house. A few days before Christmas the two servants planned to watch John Taylor to see if it was he who stole the butter. The butcher came as usual, delivered his meat and then slipped into the banqueting hall. Seeing no one he scooped two handfuls of butter, put his hands in his pockets and started to walk out. He had not walked more than three paces before the servants came out of hiding and suggested to John that he come and warm himself by the fire and have a drink of ale, as it was Christmas. He had no option but to accede to their goodwill. The fire naturally melted the butter, which ran down his trousers and into his shoes. Once one side of him was warm, they suggested he warmed the other. By this time the servants burst out laughing and poor John walked out dripping butter from his shoes. Although such an offence was punishable by death, the head of the family thought it was such a joke that he let the matter pass.

ARBOR LOW

ANCIENT MONUMENTS AND THEIR LEGENDS

On Stanton Moor is the Nine Ladies Stone Circle and the King's Stone, which date from the Bronze Age. These nine stones, approximately two feet high, are said to be nine maidens who danced to the playing of a fiddler on the sabbath. For their act of sacrilege they were turned to stone. The solitary King's Stone is said to be the fiddler.

On Chinley Churn is a barrow. According to tradition this is the resting place of an ancient chief known as 'Taro-Trin, the Bull of Conflict'.

Arbor Low Stone Circle, which is affectionately known as the 'Stonehenge of the Peak', lies just over two miles south of Monyash. It is said that the area is haunted by ghosts of the dead who were buried here after a battle many years ago. A man is recorded as saying in 1897, 'Well, you see, the folks round about never go that way at night for fear of "boggarts". Several have been seen prowling about, and it is the common talk that people must have been buried there.'

THE THREE MEN OF GARDOM'S EDGE

On Gardom's Edge, on the eastern side of Baslow, are three stone cairns in a line. There are two stories as to why these memorial stones were erected. One is that a father and his two sons were crossing this terrain and were benighted which resulted in their deaths. The other story is about three clergymen who, after attending a funeral at Eyam, returned home a little 'worse for drink'.

> 'When Ralph Rigby, twenty-two years curate of Eyam,
> was buried there, on 22nd April, 1740, three clergymen
> from Yorkshire, after attending the funeral, were lost
> on Eastmoor in the snow while returning home the same
> evening. A shepherd found one clergyman the next
> morning and restored him, but the other two perished.'

TOMB IN HARTINGTON CHURCHYARD

A gravestone in Hartington Churchyard to William Derbyshire, who died on July 28 1807, reads as follows:

> The man that lies beneath this stone
> Was for his honesty well known.
> An industrious wife he had, and children kind,
> Which gave satisfaction to his mind.
> His debts he paid — his grave you see -
> Prepare yourself to follow he.

THE TREE OF THE PEAK

The ash tree, which is so common in Derbyshire, is known as the Tree of the Peak. 'Ash' occurs in many place names in the county. Here are a few examples.

Ashbourne — Ash tree beside a stream.

Ashford in the Water — Ash beside the ford.

Monyash — Many ash trees.

One Ash Grange — One ash.

DERBYSHIRE CENTENARIANS

There have been many Derbyshire people in the past who have lived to be over one hundred years old. The champion must be a person in Taddington churchyard whose age is given as 218! Ralphe de Vernon of Sudbury, in south Derbyshire, died in 1306, at the age of 145. He was locally known as 'Sir Ranffe the Olde'. In 1831 it is recorded that living in Derbyshire were twenty-eight men and women over the age of 100. The DERBYSHIRE CHRONICLE of June 13, 1845, reported that living in Blackwell were fifteen people whose combined ages totalled 1,249 years — which meant an average age of 83. Here are some of the more renowned centenarians.

In St. Giles' Church, Matlock, can be seen the tombstone to Grace and Adam Wolley, who lived at Riber Hall. They were married in 1581, and it was not until 76 years later that the marriage was broken, with Adam's death in 1657, when he was in his hundredth year. His wife, Grace, carried on living and died in 1669 at the age of 110.

In Horsley, near Belper, in the eighteenth century lived the Bartons. It is said, 'She had twice brought into the world, and he had twice buried, the whole parish'. Frances Barton, who died in 1790 at the age of 107, was the village midwife; a job she had been doing for 80 years. Her husband was the sexton, a task he carried out for 70 years.

One of the most interesting long-livers was Sarah Rose, who died near Hope in 1819 at the age of almost 106. She was born in Glossop on May 8, 1713. The early part of her life was spent being a servant to several of the wealthy neighbouring squires. Later she married Daniel Rose of Hope, and together they had a large family. Following the death of one of her son's wives, she started to keep house for him, when she was ninety years old. This she continued to do until aged 103. At the age of 82, her eyesight was poor, her hearing was likewise, and she had lost her teeth. When 102 years of age there was a complete transformation. With her cutting her third set of teeth, her hearing came back and her eyesight was good. Two years later they declined again and she lost her teeth. At the time of her death she had 214 descendants living, and had outlived a further fifty. Like all long-livers, she indulged somewhat immoderately in narcotic weed.

On January 28, 1714, in Bamford was born George Wainwright. He lived to be 107, and rarely ever left his native Derbyshire. He was described as 'one of the most honourable, honest and trustworthy, as well as strictly moral and religious, men who ever walked, and thus he carried his years with honour to the grave.'. In 1739 he moved to Dronfield, and five years later to Totley (now part of Sheffield), which was part of Derbyshire at this time. In 1745 he married Miss Camm of Dronfield and lived in Totley, where she had twelve children. In 1791 his wife died, and he moved to live in Whiteley Woods. Finally in 1815 he went to live with a daughter in Dore, where he died on April 15, 1821. In 1810 he was chosen with fifty others to attend George the Third's Jubilee. All who attended had to be older than the King, and George Wainwright was described as being the 'King of them all'. When he was almost 100 years old the SHEFFIELD IRIS recorded in 1815 -

'We are informed that there is now living at Whiteley Wood, near this town, a man called George Wainwright, in the hundredth year of his age. He is a weaver and works at his trade, is stout and hearty, and can walk faster than most young men: he is not short of breath, but (according to our correspondent's account) is likely to live as long again as he has done.'

Following his hundredth birthday there was, every year on his birthday, a celebratory dinner, the last one being in 1821, when 53 of his descendants came. At the time of his death he had 28 grandchildren, 78 great-grandchildren and two great-great-grandchildren.

Just outside the western boundary of Derbyshire but still in the Peak District National Park is Longnor. A tombstone in the churchyard is to William Billinge who died on January 25, 1791, at the age of 112. He was a soldier and, apart from getting a musket shot in his thigh, which he called his 'French Cherry', he never had any illness during his life. He was born in a cornfield in 1679, and died in a house 150 yards away. His tombstone had the following epitaph, although the replica stone erected in 1903 has a shortened version. It is a brief outline of his life.

'Conquests I shared in many a dreadful scene,
With matchless Marlboro and with brave Eugene.
To peaceful quarters billeted am I,
And here forgetful of my labours lie.
Let me alone awhile, asleep, not slain,
And when the trumpet sounds I'll march again.'

WILLIAM BILLINGE TOMB, LONGNOR

Cornelius Crich died in 1789, aged 101. At the centenary celebrations of the glorious revolution of 1688, which was started at Revolution House in Old Whittington, near Chesterfield, Cornelius, who was born before the revolution, was carried through the streets on a chair.

Then there was Alice Buckley of Taddington, who died in 1821 aged 106, and William Congrave of Bolsover, who died in 1754 at the age of 111 — and many others.

MR. FOSTER, THE CENTENARIAN

'Foster! Thy life is spared beyond the span,
The fleeting period on the life of man.'

This special centenarian was born in Derby on November 8, 1762, and died on March 12, 1865, aged 102 years and 124 days. At the age of seventeen he joined the Derby Militia as an ensign. He served in Holland, and was in Egypt under Sir Ralph Abercrombie. He left the forces on the same day as Nelson was killed in the Battle of Trafalgar in 1805. While serving, he had shown a talent for painting, an occupation he now carried out. His work was well received, and he became the 'Miniature Painter to the Royal Family'. He was given apartments in the Round Tower at Windsor Castle, and while there he frequently played whist with the Royal circle. Apart from the Royal family, he drew portraits of the leading people of the day, including Lord Byron and Sir Walter Scott. In May 1811 in the MACCLESFIELD COURIER appeared the following poem about Foster, by the poet Ramsay:

'First from the shadow on the polish'd wall

Were took those faces which profile we call;

The first was drawn by the Corinthian dame,

Who, by the art, immortalised her name;

From posture next improving on her plan,

The artist with the pencil took the man;

Yet oft the lines where blemishes prevail'd,

Were taught to flatter, and the likeness fail'd.

But how to form machines to take the face

With nice precision in one minute space;

To paint with bold, unerring certainty

The face profile, in shades that time defy,

Where all allow the likeness to agree,

This honour, Foster, was reserved for thee.'

Later in life he published educational charts, such as 'A Chronological Chart of the History of the British Empire'. He was a fairly small man, standing some 5 feet 4 inches tall. He is said to have had a fair complexion, and been active in both body and soul. He married five times and was father to seventeen children. Upon his death his last daughter, Phyllis Howard Foster, was aged thirteen. Because of his many marriages, he was often ridiculed, and one lady penned the following:

'Mr. Foster married a wife, and then he lost her;
He married a second, and then a third,
And then a fourth, upon my word!
Laugh not, good sirs, for I protest,
A fifth is added to the rest,
And a fair daughter calls him sire
At fivescore years. You must admire
My tale, if true –
Why, Sir, I mean five score and two!'

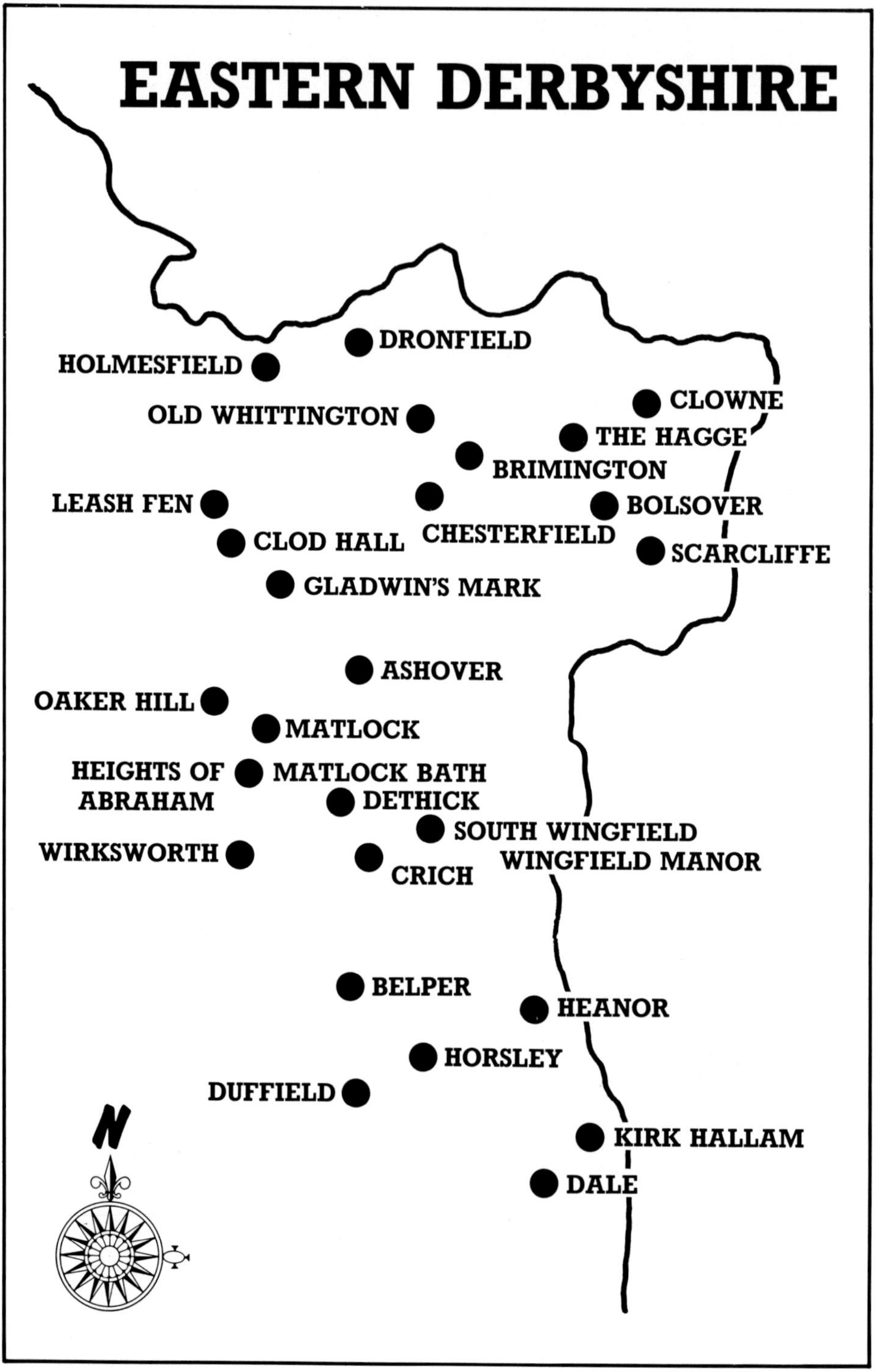

EASTERN DERBYSHIRE

DRONFIELD

HOLMESFIELD

CLOWNE

OLD WHITTINGTON

THE HAGGE

BRIMINGTON

LEASH FEN

BOLSOVER

CLOD HALL CHESTERFIELD

SCARCLIFFE

GLADWIN'S MARK

ASHOVER

OAKER HILL

MATLOCK

HEIGHTS OF MATLOCK BATH
ABRAHAM DETHICK

SOUTH WINGFIELD

WIRKSWORTH WINGFIELD MANOR

CRICH

BELPER

HEANOR

HORSLEY

DUFFIELD

KIRK HALLAM

DALE

N

EASTERN DERBYSHIRE

OAKER HILL

'Tis said that to the brow of yon fair hill
Two brothers climb, and turning face from face
Not one more look exchanging, grief to still
Or feed, each planted on that lofty place
A chosen tree: then eager to fulfil
Their course, like two new-born rivers, they
In opposite direction urged their way
Down from the far-seen mount. No blast might kill
Or blight that fond memorial: the trees grew
And now entwine their arms: but ne'er again
Embraced these brothers upon earth's wide plain:
Nor aught of mutual joy or sorrow knew
Until their spirits mingled in the sea
That to itself takes all — eternity.'

William Wordsworth

Lying some two miles north west of Matlock is this prominent isolated hill. Crowning the summit is one solitary sycamore tree. The current legends differ slightly from Wordsworth's account above. The two brothers climbed to the top and both planted a tree before going their separate ways. One brother succeeded in life and his tree flourished, the other did not and his tree died. To confuse the issue, I have found two other tales concerning the single tree. One is that a tree was planted on the top to honour King George the Fifth's coronation in 1911. The other is that a man named Shore, which is a local name of the area, planted two sycamores. His idea was that following his death the trees were to be cut down and his coffin was to be made out of the wood. Personally I like the two brothers' version. It is the most romantic, if the least plausible.

THE WISEST MAN IN MATLOCK

George Twyford, who was known as the 'wisest man in Matlock', died in January 1875. He was a total eccentric, who made sufficient money during the tourist season to keep him for the rest of the year. He was principally a beggar and a 'musician' who was known all over this region of Derbyshire.

> 'His persistence in following people about, his rude music, and his even ruder attempts at singing, added to his strange gyrations and antics, as he every now and again attempted to break into step, gained for him that "plenty of money".

As you may gather, although somewhat daft in his mannerisms, he had a cute intelligence, to which the following two stories bear witness.

As usual he followed a couple who seemed likely to give him some money for his foolery. He went through his act of dancing, singing and curtseying. Eventually the woman turned to her husband and said, 'Poor fellow! Give him a shilling, dear; he's silly!' George was duly given a shilling and replied, 'Thank yer! I've getten a brother a' home that's sillier nor mey!'

He then left the couple continuing to sing his favourite verse, which he always sang to people, which was -

> 'The wisest man in Matlock,
> Rice pudding with bricks in -
> Pudding dipped in brandy.'

Another time he was following two men and once again going through his party piece, hoping for some money so that he would leave them alone. At length one of them decided to give George a penny, and just as he was about to do so his friend said, 'Why, he wouldn't have sense enough to know a sixpence from a penny if you offered them to him!' His companion withdrew the money and placed a sixpence and a penny on his hand, and, as an experiment, he told George he could have his choice. Without any hesitation George replied, 'Ah wunna bi greydey! I'll tak' th' little 'un!' While the two men reflected, George walked away!

THE HEIGHTS OF ABRAHAM

Why the Heights of Abraham (Matlock Bath) were so named is, alas, no romantic tale. An officer who had fought with General Wolfe came here in the late eighteenth century. He thought they were very similar to the Heights of Abraham in Quebec in Canada, and since then the name has stuck.

In about 1840 a person carved on the rocks there -

'He who climbs these heights sublime,
Will wish to come a second time.'.

Later a different carver added two more lines -

'And when he comes a second time,
I hope he'll make a better rhyme.'

TOMB INSIDE ASHOVER CHURCH

To the memory
of
DAVID WALL
Whose superior performance
on the bassoon
Endeared him
to an extensive musical
acquaintance.
His social life closed on
the 4 of December, 1796
in his 57 year.'

ASHOVER CHURCH

THE DAY THE GROUND OPENED

In the Ashover parish registers is the following entry -

'1660 — Dorothy Mately, supposed wife of John Flint
of this parish, forswore herself, whereupon the
ground opened, and she sunk over head 23rd March
and being found dead, she was buried 25th March.'

Dorothy Mately worked in the nearby lead mines, generally washing and sieving the rubbish
for any lead ore. She was renowned for her uncouth behaviour — swearing, cursing, lying
and thieving. After she had fully elaborated her innocence over a specific accusation she
would usually say, 'I would I might sink into the earth if it be so.'. John Bunyan relates her story
in THE LIFE AND DEATH OF MR. BADMAN, which he published in the late seventeenth
century, and the following is extracted from it.

76

'Now upon the 23rd of March 1660, this Dorothy was washing of ore upon the top of a steep hill about a quarter of a mile from Ashover, and was there taxed by a lad for taking of two single pence out of his pocket (for he had laid his breeches by, and was at work in his drawers), but she violently denied it, wishing the ground might swallow her up if she had them.'

But behold, they had not got above ten yards from Dorothy but they heard her crying for help, so, looking back, he saw the woman and her tub and sieve, twisting round, and sinking in the ground. 'Then', said the man, 'pray to God to pardon thy sin, for thou art never like to be seen alive any longer.' So she and her tub twirled round and round, till they sank about three yards into the earth, and there for a while stayed. Then she called for help again, thinking, as she said, she would stay there. Now the man, though greatly amazed, did begin to think which way to help her; but immediately a great stone, which appeared in the earth, fell upon her head and broke her skull, and then the earth fell in upon her and covered her.

She was afterwards dug up and found about four yards within the ground, and the boy's two pence in her pocket, but her tub and sieve could not be found.'

Being a lead-mining area, the ground would have been honeycombed with shafts and passageways and, therefore, most unstable. This would seem to have been the reason why the ground collapsed under her, although one could say that it was justice done!

DETHICK CHURCH

A DETHICK TALE

South east of Matlock is the small farming hamlet of Dethick, which is just a cluster of houses beside an imposing church. Born in the village was Anthony Babington, who was one of the ring leaders of the ill-fated Babington Plot to release Mary Queen of Scots from nearby Wingfield Manor. However, this tale concerns a man who died in about 1850. He was the clerk to Dethick church and always made a habit of going to all the nearby wakes and fairs, for he could play both the pipe and fiddle.

The story told about him concerns his visit to Ashover feast. The attendance was very large and he began to wonder where he was going to sleep. In the early part of the evening he slipped away and took up residence in one of the inn's bedrooms, securing himself a bed for the night. Later that evening there was a knock on the door, and in a deep voice he asked what they wanted. 'Oh, they said, we want to come to bed, of course.' Creating as much noise as possible, he told them it was full in there. 'Why, who have you got inside?' they enquired. 'Who?' he cried, 'The Clerk o' Dethick, the piper o' Lea, old England's fiddler, Billy Bunting and me!' On hearing this they moved on to seek other accommodation!

CRICH CHURCH

THE FAREWELL ADDRESS OF THE VICAR OF CRICH

On Sunday, August 27th 1837 the congregation dutifully attended church at Crich to be met with the following surprise announcement from the vicar.

"Tomorrow, my friends, this living will be vacant, and if any of you is desirous of becoming my successor, he has now an opportunity. Let him use his influence, and who can tell but he may be honoured with the title of "Vicar of Crich". As this is my last address, I shall only say, had I been a blacksmith, or a son of Vulcan, the following lines might not have been inappropriate.

My sledge and hammer lie reclined,
My bellows, too, have lost their wind,
My fire's extinct, my forge decay'd,
And in the dust my vice is laid.
My coal is spent, my iron's gone,
My nails are drove, my work is done;
My fire-dried corpse lies here at rest,
And, smoke-like, sears up to be bless'd.

If you expect anything more, you are deceived; for I shall only say, 'Friends, farewell, farewell!'

ABRAHAM JAMES OF SOUTH WINGFIELD

Abraham James was born in South Wingfield on December 22, 1799. His father, Joseph, was the village schoolmaster but unfortunately he died young and his son was left to be brought up by his mother with no opportunity for schooling. As soon as he was old enough he worked on a stocking-frame. In his early twenties he began to realise that he was at a disadvantage at being unable to write, and so set about teaching himself. He wrote the following on May 19, 1844 — as an apology for bad writing.

> I never went a day to school,
> To learn the art to control
> My pen, when I attempt to write,
> Or else you know perhaps I might
> Have learnt the art as well as you,
> Though my capacities are few;
> What makes me worse, I have no skill,
> To make a pen if I'd a quill.

As you can see, he was also a bit of a poet.

He soon married Elizabeth Turner, a girl from the village. Her brother was a stonemason and persuaded Abraham that there was a better living from this work than working at a stocking-frame. Showing the same application to his new trade as to his writing, he soon became a very capable stonemason.

He also kept a record of all the births and deaths of his neighbours, and kept a diary of special events which occurred in the village and surroundings. On sending a pair of shoes to be repaired, he enclosed the following poem to the shoemaker:

> John Bunting, you these shoes must mend,
> And have them done by the week's end;
> The soles and heels you must repair,
> And make them me quite fit to wear.
>
> In working use the best of leather;
> Be sure to sew them well together,
> And when you've made these shoes complete,
> Be honest and do not me cheat.
>
> With reason you must set the price,
> You shall not have to ask for't twice;
> Thus you'll oblige him who remains
> Your humble servant, Abraham James.

He was a very keen gardener and his garden was always kept immaculate. Regrettably this self-taught bard died aged 65 on June 6, 1864. The following are four entries from his record of events.

A most terrible hailstorm, which broke nearly £100 worth of windows in the village, and did several thousand pounds damage in the parish. The corn was nearly all destroyed, scarcely an ear left standing; vast quantities of little birds were killed. Many of the hailstones which fell were as large as pigeons' eggs, and some were larger than geese eggs; and notwithstanding the excessive heat of the sun, they lay upon the ground four days, before they melted. This mournful visitation happened on Saturday, 1st July 1826, between 5 and 6 o'clock in the evening.

A fiery meteor seen at the time the moon was eclipsed. 26th January 1823.

A great earthquake happened 17th March 1816.

Four men hanged at Derby, for burning Mr. Halton's stacks, 15th August 1817.

WINGFIELD MANOR

Wingfield Manor lies just south of South Wingfield. The ruined building, which dates back to 1441, was once owned by the Earls of Shrewsbury, and here the captive Mary Queen of Scots was imprisoned. According to a legend, the very old walnut tree, which collapsed in 1973, grew from a walnut dropped by Antony Babington, the leader of the famous Babington Plot to free Mary. It is said that when he came to visit Mary Queen of Scots in 1586 in secret, he painted his face with walnut oil as a disguise. The tree grew on the site of Mary's apartments.

CLOD HALL

On the lonely high road which crosses between Leash Fen and Birchen Edge, east of Baslow, is Clod Hall Farm (Grid Ref.SK296726). According to a tradition, a man hanged himself on a tree in close proximity to the Hall that is built there today. The nearby villages of Brampton and Baslow at first would not agree to bury his body. Eventually Baslow agreed, and the villages built a clod (turf) hut and kept a smoky fire going in it for twenty-four hours. They then buried the body and claimed some land for their labour.

GLADWIN'S MARK

Marked on the one inch Ordnance Survey Tourist map of the Peak District at Grid Reference SK306667, and lying some three miles due east of Rowsley, is Gladwin's Mark. There is a tale in its name.

Long before there were any field boundaries, this moorland area of Derbyshire was only crossed by the odd footpath and track. It was a place that was infrequently traversed, for it was a bleak region where few cared to linger. One afternoon late in December when a thick layer of snow covered the landscape, a man named Gladwin set off to cross the area. Before he was halfway across the weather deteriorated, a snow storm blew up and darkness fell. He reached a cairn and decided to wait till the morning so that he could see his way ahead. The night was bitterly cold, and fearing he would lose his life through exposure he began dismantling the cairn. For the rest of the night until dawn he worked, dismantling and then rebuilding the cairn, keeping his mind active and his body warm through exertion. With the coming light he relaxed, for he knew he had cheated death. He set off and completed his journey. Ever since the stone cairn there has been named after his ordeal.

HOLMESFIELD

THE HOLMESFIELD GHOST

Towards the latter end of the nineteenth century the locals of Holmesfield would tell you tales of a ghost who appeared at midnight on Millthorpe Lane. The ghost sat astride a white horse. One day three of the boys from the village decided that they would stay up late to see if they could catch a glimpse of the ghost. News of their plans soon spread through the village. Around eleven thirty in the evening with no moon in the sky, the three boys, armed with sticks, walked stealthily down the lane. Part way down, to their horror, they saw a white horse. Immediately they dropped their sticks and ran home as fast as they could. It was learnt later that one of the farmers, learning of their plan, decided to play a practical joke and tethered a white horse there.

On another occasion late at night, the same three boys were leaning against the wall of the George and Dragon Inn. The night was a wild one, with wind sprift cloud and a full moon. The light from the moon shone through the stained glass windows of the church and danced on a white tomb. Naturally the boys thought this was the ghost. Moments later a clattering noise was heard from the churchyard. They could bear it no longer and hurriedly departed to the sanctuary of their homes. Later they learnt that once again they had succumbed to a practical joke. One of the tombstones was new and very white. The clattering noise had been made by a dog who was trailing a couple of chains fastened to his collar.

A ghost in Dronfield was supposed to haunt Cemetery Road. Like the Holmesfield ghost, it was a figment of the imagination. The local policeman decided to investigate the stories, and so late at night took up a secluded position overlooking the road and waited. Minutes later the ghost appeared. He quickly rushed at it and grabbed the white figure. Removing the sheet, he found he had caught his son, who with his friends had concocted the whole idea!

82

CARTLEDGE HALL

THE QUARRELLING BROTHERS

In Holmesfield is the interesting early seventeenth century building known as Cartledge Hall. In the eighteenth century the house was occupied by two brothers who continually argued. The younger brother always bore the brunt of the argument. One day, while they were arguing, the younger brother heard music coming from another room. To the surprise of his brother he left abruptly and raced to the room from where he believed the sound had come. He found nobody and could see nothing, but a voice spoke to him saying –

"Thy duty is to leave this place and build a house elsewhere".

The voice is believed to have been that of a fairy. The younger brother left and built a new house on the opposite side of the road, blocking his brother's view!

FOUR LANE ENDS

RAISING THE DEVIL

A man from Holmesfield, near the southern boundary of Sheffield, decided to call the Devil. At dusk, and armed with a frying-pan and a key, he went to a nearby 'four lane-ends'. Here many people gathered to watch the proceedings. The man rattled both the frying-pan and the key together. While he did so he chanted the following lines over and over.

> I raised the Devil, and the Devil raised me,
> I never shall forget when the Devil raised me.

After a few minutes there was a loud clap of thunder and the Devil appeared, although only the man saw him. Without waiting for the Devil to speak, the Holmesfield man said,

> "Get thee behind me Satan, for it is written that thou shalt worship the Lord thy God, and Him only
> shalt thou serve".

The Devil vanished and was not seen again.

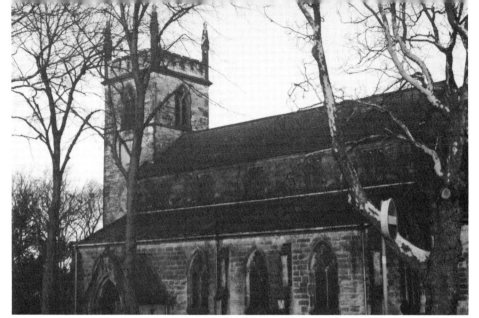

BRIMINGTON CHURCH

A BRIMINGTON CHARACTER

Living on Brimington Common near Chesterfield in the nineteenth century was an elderly woman known as Old Martha. Two stories are told about her. One is that one day a man saw her and, for a bit of fun, he suggested that they get married in Brimington Church, naming the date and time. News of this proposal spread through the village, and on the appointed day a large crowd gathered at the church entrance to watch. Old Martha arrived on time, dressed in a new black suit with a fancy lace blouse underneath. She waited but her man never appeared, to her dismay and the crowd's delight, who were now in full swing with their gibes and jokes. There were also a good number in sympathy with her, shocked at such treatment of a lady over seventy. But Martha proved to be best in self-defence, and left after giving the hecklers a piece of strong language.

The other story concerns the opening of the new cemetery. Old Martha was asked whether she would like to be buried in the new or the old. She replied that she did not really mind which. If she was placed in the new one she would at least have fresh air; if she was placed in the old one she would have company!

CHESTERFIELD'S CROOKED SPIRE

Whichever way you turn your eye,
It always seems to be awry:
Pray, can you tell the reason why?
The only reason known of weight,
Is that the thing was never straight;
Nor know the people where to go,
To find the man to make it so;
Since none can furnish such a plan,
Except a perfect upright man:
So that the spire, 'tis very plain,
For ages crooked must remain;
And while it stands must ever be,
An emblem of deformity.
(Author unknown)

The spire was built at the end of the fourteenth century and its height is 228 feet. It seems probable that the timbers used were green, and when the heat of the sun dried them out one of the main supports split, tilting the spire. It leans almost eight feet, but is decidedly safe. The eight sides of the spire are flat, but because the lead plates are placed in herringbone style, the effect of the spire's lean is accentuated.

Various legends surround the spire, and one is that the lean was made by the Devil who watched very annoyed as the spire was built. Another says that the first couple to be married in the church were so innocent that the steeple crooked. It is said that the next innocent pair to be married there will cause the spire to straighten itself again.

Another story as to why the spire is crooked tells of the Devil, who frequently passed overhead on his way to Nottingham. He was working so hard getting up to all sorts of mischief in Nottingham that he grew weary with his effort. Late one night he was hurrying once more to Nottingham but he was really too tired. He did not look where he was going, and before he knew what was happening he had bumped into the spire. That is why the spire is bent!

LEECH FEND

LEECH FEND

When Chesterfield was heath and broom,
Leech Fend was a market town;
Now Leech Fend is all heath and broom,
And Chesterfield a market town.

An old saying.

The legend of Leech Fend is probably the oldest one of Derbyshire. For generations people have recalled the saying. Looking on the Ordance Survey map today you will see, three miles east of Curbar and on the edge of the Peak District National Park, an area of very flat moorland known as Leash Fen. It is this extremely boggy area to which the legend refers. Here before the first century A.D. stood an Ancient Briton settlement of wooden huts roofed with rushes. One night, according to the legend, the earth opened and swallowed the complete village. In the nineteenth century, the Duke of Rutland had a ditch dug across the fen to help drain the land. Sure enough, the workmen engaged on this found large quantities of pottery and black oak.

TOMB IN BOLSOVER CHURCHYARD

BOLSOVER CHURCH

Here lies
in a horizontal position
the outside case of
THOMAS HINDE
Clock and Watch maker.
Who departed this life wound up
in hope of being taken in hand
by his Maker and being
thoroughly cleaned, repaired and
set a-going in the world to come
On the 15th of August 1836
In the 19th year of his life.

This is certainly a cheerful epitaph for someone who had an untimely end.

CLOWNE CHURCH

Clowne Church, which is dedicated to St. John the Baptist, dates from Norman times and lies one and a half miles south-east of Barlborough. The church stands on its own away from the village, on the eastern side of a minor road. It is said that it was spirited across the road to its new position.

THE GHOST OF HAGG

The Hagge, a very fine Jacobean house near Staveley, was built in 1630 by Sir Peter Frecheville, as a shooting lodge. According to this old couplet, the house has a ghost.

> Then as you cross the entrance hall to ascend the oaken stair
> Fear not to meet the lady who oft-times lingers there.
> In cloak and hat of antique guise, and robes of purest white,
> She vanishes from the gazer's eyes e'en in the moontide light.

On one occasion a visitor was staying at the house, and at breakfast he asked his host, "Is the lady in white, whom I passed on the stairs last night, coming for breakfast?" His host had to gently inform his guest that he had seen the ghost!

THE MANDRAKE TREE

A mandrake tree is said to have been growing last century at The Hagge (Hagge Farm), which lies one and a half miles north-east of New Whittington, at Grid Reference SK413766. The mandrake tree is rare in Britain, and its long-forked root is said to resemble a demon or human body. Moreover, if anyone breaks a piece off this tree it will moan as though a demon is talking.

Before this particular mandrake existed a ghost was frequently seen here, and when this ghost was laid the tree was planted. In time the mandrake became a curiosity and quite a tourist attraction. It was finally decided to fell it, but because the tree moaned so much the only way to uproot it seemed to be by using a dog. The dog was tied to the tree and a large piece of meat was placed just out of his reach, the idea being that the dog would become so ravenous that he would pull the tree out in his attempts to reach the meat. The tree was blown down in 1883.

LADY CONSTANTIA

SCARCLIFFE CHURCH

In Scarcliffe Church in north-east Derbyshire is a marble tombstone to Lady Constantia de Frechville, who died about A.D. 1200. The engraving shows her clutching her baby. According to the legend, she fell in love and conceived a child but her lover would not marry her. After giving birth to the child she fled the area and rode into Scarcliffe Wood. The trees were so dense that she lost her way, and if it had not been for the tolling of the Curfew Bell in Scarcliffe Church she and her child would have perished in the wood. The bell guided her back to safety. Upon her death, in her Will, she allotted five acres of land to pay for the Curfew Bell to be rung for six weeks each year ever after. These have been the three weeks before and three weeks after Christmas. However, since the last war the bell has remained unrung.

HEANOR

EDWARD STAINSBY — THE HEANOR RUNNER

Edward Stainsby was born on January 11 1825, and of the first nineteen years of his life very little is known. He was a real jack-of-all-trades, for he worked as a framework-knitter, a footrunner, a lace-maker, labourer, navvy, greengrocer, collier and a hawker of fish, shrimps, mussels, oysters and crabs! It was at the age of nineteen that his natural talent became known. A prize race was being held locally, and he went along to watch. One of the runners approached him and asked if he would hold his clothes while he ran the race. Edward agreed, but at the start of the race, instead of watching, he joined in and won the race with considerable ease and still holding the clothes! Naturally this performance did not go unnoticed and Edward was soon being trained.

His first race, over a mile distance, took place on Plough Monday, 1845. He won confidently. That same year he beat the best runners from Arnold, Carlton, Derby, Hucknall, Basford, Sheffield, Macclesfield and Gorton. Not only was he unsurpassed at running but he was also extremely good at hurdling and vaulting. He also often took part in wheelbarrow, donkey and pony races. At the Heanor races, in 1864, he won the donkey race on his own donkey, Jenny Lind. The prize was a pound. The same day he rode another race against one other for a new bridle. Edward was six feet tall, and standing astride his donkey he did not need to rest his weight on the donkey, whereas his competitor could not reach the ground with his feet. As a result, during the race, which Edward won, he could give the donkey a rest and run astride it! The other donkey was known as Lord Byron's Devil.

> As the loud huzzas arise,
> Jenny bears away the prize.

A little later he sold his favourite donkey -

> He sold his darling Jenny,
> And a pony bought.

When asked where he was going to keep his new animal, Edward replied, 'By jingo, it nivver entered my head that it ud ivver want owt to eat!'

Edward's nickname was Rabbie, but why this name no-one knows. In his forties he entered his last race, a mile heat. The four other runners were much younger than he. He ran in fine style and came third, but he was so out of breath that it was several minutes before he could talk. When he did, he gasped, 'Now I know that I'm not so young as I used to be.'.

EDWARD PRINCE OF HEANOR

Living at Heanor, where he was born on March 4, 1800, was Edward Prince. He was the fourth son of a stocking-maker, and because of his small size he was nicknamed 'Little Neddy'. His other brothers and sisters, eleven in all, were all normal and very healthy. Edward grew normally until the age of seven, when suddenly he stopped developing both physically and mentally: he was left small and immature. Even when he was in his fifties you would see him on the street playing with the other children at marbles or some other game. He went to school and learnt how to read, but he was not able to master any of the other subjects. He later joined his father and became a stocking-maker. His father had to make a special small frame, and it took many years of patience to teach him how to operate it efficiently. He worked at this until he was forty-five years of age.

There are two stories told about him. One is that he was a great lover of pipe smoking and rarely would you see him without a pipe in his mouth. He was also very cunning, for if anyone went up to him and said, 'Neddy, gie us a bit o' baccy', he would immediately pull out an empty pouch. The asker would see he had none and would have compassion and give him some of his own. Unknown to the enquirer, Neddy always carried two pouches. One he had filled with his tobacco and the other was always empty to show the scroungers! He also carried a selection of pipes, and as many as four would be seen in his breast pocket.

The other story gives an example of his great determination to keep a resolution. A group of people decided it was time that Edward had a new suit. However, they stipulated that in return he should not smoke for a year. 'Just let me smoke one more pipeful and I will agree', said Neddy. True to his word, he relinquished his pipes and pouches to the group to keep for a year. Although frequently teased at not smoking during that year, it is to his credit that he never once smoked.

KIRK HALLAM CHURCH

OLD PATRICK RICE

In Kirk Hallam, which lies west of Ilkeston on the eastern boundary of the county, in the eighteenth century lived a village character named Patrick Rice. Inside the church one can see his epitaph, which he wrote two years before he actually died in 1766. He also made other preparations for his eventual departure by ordering his coffin two years before time. On delivery he kept the coffin beside his bed, and, until he occupied it forever, he stored his best clothes in it!

DALE CHURCH

DALE HERMITAGE

0 Deepdale! lovely is thy land,
With pasturing herd and flock;
And lovely is thine Hermitage,
Cut in the solid rock.

From 'The Legend of Dale Abbey'
by R. Howitts

Both Dale Abbey and Hermitage lie some seven miles east of Derby. According to the legend, Cornelius, a hard-working baker from the parish of St. Mary in Derby made the Hermitage. He was 'a religious man, fearing the Lord and much intent upon sins and good works'. One day he fell asleep, and during a dream the Virgin Mary came to him and told him to leave his bakery business and live a life of solitude in Deepdale. He did not know the place, but he did as he was bidden, set off and was guided to the Dale. Here, about the year 1130, he cut his dwelling out of rock, complete with a doorway and two windows. One day he made a fire and the smoke drifted high into the sky and was seen by Ranulphus, the son of Geremund, the Lord of Ockbrook. When he reached the Hermitage he was overcome with compassion, seeing the hermit's simple way of life. He granted the hermit the site he had chosen and also the tithe from the mill at Borrowash.

The surroundings to the Hermitage are interesting. The nearby well is called Hermitage Well, and the farmhouse passed on approaching the Hermitage is unusual in sharing a roof with the church. Despite the joint roof the farmhouse was once an inn, while the church holds the sacred Abbey font.

93

DALE ABBEY WINDOW

DALE ABBEY

'With that one arch before thee set -
That one old abbey-window fair;
The only wreck of the rich fame
That restless time would spare.'

From 'The Legend of Dale Abbey'
by R. Howitts

There are two legends as to how Dale Abbey came to be built here in 1204. The first states that the King granted to the Prior, St. Robert, as much land as he could encircle with a plough between sunrise and sunset. The plough was to be pulled by two deer caught locally. This he did, as depicted on the stained glass windows which were removed from the Abbey when it was dissolved in 1539 and are now placed in Morley Church, some four miles away. As mentioned in the poem only a solitary window archway, forty feet high and sixteen feet wide, stands forlornly in a field on the site of the Abbey.

The other version says that the site was determined by a vision. One Uthlagus, 'a very famous man', was sitting on a hill to the west of the future Abbey. He fell asleep and dreamed of a golden cross standing on the site of the Abbey. Later the Abbey was built in that position.

DUFFIELD CHURCH

On looking at the map of Duffield, you will note that Duffield's church is well away from the village — about half a mile south of it. According to a tradition this was the work of the Devil. The church was to be built near to the ruined castle. The materials were gathered there and the workmen started, but when they returned the following day all their work had been pulled down and removed to the present site. The same thing happened each night for a week, and the workmen were getting annoyed at continually starting the building from scratch each morning. A few days later they gave up and commenced work where the stones had been placed by the Devil overnight. From that moment onwards their work was never hindered, and they built the present church. It is said that the Devil's reason for removing the site from near the castle was because, had it been built on the lofty position near the castle, the church would have attracted too many customers!

Inside the church is an unusual tomb to Anthony Bradshaw. He had the tomb made fourteen years before he died. Part of the information on the tombstone should have been updated, for it records his two wives and a mere twenty children. However, before he died, he fathered a further three children. In his Will he left money for an almshouse to be built for four elderly women of Duffield. They were to use his pew in the church and to keep his tomb dusted for ever. The almshouses have long since been pulled down but, from the money from the sale of the land, four elderly ladies in the village each receive a small sum of money from the interest, half yearly. They still carry out the custom and dust his tomb as requested.

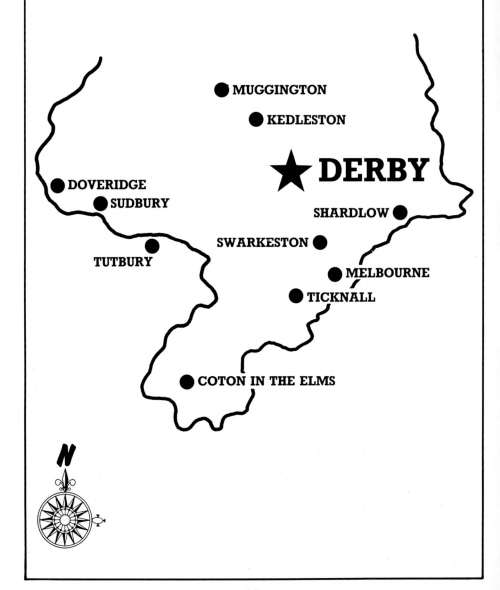

DERBY
AND
SOUTH DERBYSHIRE

MUGGINGTON

KEDLESTON

★ DERBY

DOVERIDGE

SUDBURY

SHARDLOW

SWARKESTON

TUTBURY

MELBOURNE

TICKNALL

COTON IN THE ELMS

N

DERBY AND SOUTH DERBYSHIRE

THE DERBY RAM

The origin of this renowned legend is not known. The following are several verses from one of the versions of the ballad.

First verse -

As I was going to Derby, Sir,
All on a market day,
I met the finest Ram, Sir,
That ever was fed on hay.

Chorus —
Dddle-i-day, daddle-i-day,
Fal-de-ral, fal-de-ral, daddle-i-day.

This Ram was fat behind, Sir,
This Ram was fat before,
This Ram was ten yards high, Sir,
Indeed he was no more.

The wool upon his belly, Sir,
It dragged upon the ground,
It was sold in Derby town, Sir,
For forty thousand pound.

The space between his horns, Sir,
Was as far as man could reach,
And there they built a pulpit,
For the Parson there to preach.

The teeth that were in his mouth, Sir,
Were like a regiment of men,
And the tongue that hung between them, Sir,
Would have dined them twice and again.

And of this tail so long, Sir,
'Twas ten miles and an ell,
They made a goodly rope, Sir,
To toll the market bell.

This Ram had four legs to walk on, Sir,
This Ram had four legs to stand,
And every leg he had, Sir,
Stood on an acre of land.

The butcher that killed this Ram, Sir,
Was drowned in the blood,
And the boy that held the pail, Sir,
Was carried away in the flood.

Final verse -

Indeed, Sir, this is true, Sir,
I never was taught to lie,
And had you been to Derby, Sir,
You'd have seen it as well as I.

DERBYSHIRE'S STRONG MAN

Living in Derby in about 1735 was Thomas Topham. He was famous for his Herculean strength, and was said to be able to break a thick broomstick by simply hitting it against his bare arm. Among the many other stories about him, he was capable of lifting two hogshead of water (which would weigh about half a ton), he could carry a house beam on his shoulder, and at a turnpike gate he could heave his own horse over!

The people of Derby were sceptical of these stories, and so Topham decided to give a demonstration of his strength. He charged them a shilling a head. He had to see Alderman Cooper for permission to hold the demonstration. The Alderman, on hearing what Topham was going to do, asked him to take off his shirt so that he could see this unusually strong man. Everywhere was a mass of rippling muscle and he stood 5 feet 10 inches tall. The Alderman noticed he walked with a slight limp. Topham explained that he once wagered that three horses could not move him from a post he had wrapped his legs round. Before he was ready, the whip was cracked, the three horses pulled, and he broke his thigh.

These are some of his feats at the demonstration.

He rolled up a pewter dish weighing half a stone as an ordinary man would roll up a sheet of paper.

He held out a pewter quart vessel at arm's length and squeezed in its sides till they met — like an eggshell.

He lifted 200 pounds with his little finger.

He broke a rope, fastened to the floor, that would sustain
a ton weight.

He lifted a table of oak, six feet long, with half a
hundredweight attached to its more distant end, with
his teeth and the two near legs being placed on his
knees for leverage.

Mr. Chambers, Vicar of All Saints, weighed 27 stone.
He laid his head on one chair and his feet on another.
Topham lifted him off both chairs with one hand.

Four men, totalling 56 stone in weight, sat on his chest.
He heaved up and down at pleasure.

He struck a round iron bar of an inch diameter against
his naked arm and bent it like a bow with a single
stroke.

To complete the demonstration, which had proved beyond doubt that he possessed
phenomenal strength, he sang a solo, 'Mad Tom', and his voice was said to be 'more terrible
than sweet'.

Here is one final story about him. He had a room at the Virgin's Inn in Derby, and he had a row
with the inn-keeper. This was unusual, for he was known as a gentle person who went out of
his way to avoid conflict. However, it does have its humorous side. Topham took the iron spit
from the mantlepiece and tied it round the inn-keeper's neck. He made sure that the fellow
could not lift it over his head, and the man therefore had no option but to wear it until it was
removed!

PIN TOMMY

Walking the street of Derby in the 1830s was a most unusual character known as Pin Tommy.
He had a mania for collecting pins. Any that he found or was given were quickly added to his
clothing. The pins were pinned to his trousers' legs, waistcoat and coat and, with several
thousand attached, it was as though he wore a suit of armour. He prided himself on his
collection and was never known to part with a single pin. When he was starving he went
begging for food, and this was a typical encounter.

> 'Yes, Tommy, here's something for you — but you'll give
> me a pin, won't you?'
>
> 'No, aw shanna! What nun I gey thy a pin for?
> If thar wants one tha mun goo and get one!'

He would rather go hungry than part with just one pin from his huge collection. Alas, this is all
we know of him, and what happened to both himself and his pins I cannot discover.

BIG EATERS

People who can consume large quantities of food are fortunately among the minority, and here are just three of the Derbyshire 'big eaters'.

Living in Derby in the last century was a huge strong man named Hudson. Because of his immense size and strength he worked as a striker in one of the town's iron works. Every day his meal consisted of a leg of mutton and a four pound loaf of bread. The mutton was cooked to his liking, just warm and very rare. Since his family increased and he was not earning enough at the iron works to feed both his children and himself, the family emigrated to America. There, it is said, he earned sufficient money to do both.

Born in Nottingham in 1768, Jacky Peet later became resident in Derbyshire. For breakfast he always ate a couple of rabbits, and only once was he ever known to admit he was full. On that occasion he ate a bucketful of broth as his soup and, for his sweet, a plum pudding of massive proportions. He often went to the Nottingham Goose Fair, and once he sneaked into a friend's larder there. With all the food around him, he sat on the floor and simply gorged himself. He was so fat after this that he could not fit through the door and had no option but to await discovery by his friends!

It is recorded that on May 3, 1777, Ralph Oakley sat down in the Red Lion Inn, in Stanton-by-Dale, which is just east of Derby. Here a record was kept by the parish clerk and four others, who watched him eat the following meal within the space of one hour -

First Course — 2 qts. milk, 30 eggs, half a pound of sugar,
3 penny loaves, a small amount of ginger and
nutmeg and 1 oz. mustard. The whole lot
was boiled together.
Second Course — A piece of cheese and a pound of boiled
bacon.
Third Course — Half a pound fried bacon, 1 penny loaf,
1 quart ale, one and a half pennysworth
gingerbread and a pint of ale to finish.
Fourth Course — A custard weighing 2 lbs., 1 oz. mustard,
some pepper as the sauce to it, mixed with
with a pint of new milk.
Fifth Course — To complete the meal he drank 3 pints of ale.

Having consumed the above, he was challenged to a 300 yard race. His opponent was a young man named Windley. He accepted the challenge and won the race by 12 yards. As recorded, he returned to the Red Lion and carried on drinking for another two hours.

DOG TAX

Early in 1753 a report was published whose conclusions were that dogs should be taxed. A few days later the Derby newspaper, on April 6 1753, included the following advertisement.

'Whereas, by a late report has been an Act that all dogs are to be taxed. This is to give notice, that those persons who will hang their dogs, and bring the skins to Mr. Jonathan Kendal's, near S. Wingfield, on Monday, the 16th of April; to Richard Redfern's, at Haynor, the 17th, and to the King's Head at Derby, the 20th; shall receive for every skin not less than 2s.6d.(12.5p); and every mastiff or large mongrel — 5s.0d.(25p); to be clean taken off, and without slits, ready money.'

THE MEN WHO NEVER WERE

The following are two true stories of women who wore men's clothes, did men's jobs and married other women.

Harriet Bridget Moore, alias John Murphy:

When Harriet was only about ten years of age, her mother died in 1816. Left an orphan, she had to seek work, and decided to dress as a youth as this was safer for her and gave her more chance of employment. She called herself John Murphy, Murphy being her mother's maiden name. She worked as a cabin boy before becoming a foot boy to a Reverend Duke. Here she stayed for a year, but eventually had to leave as one of his maids had fallen in love with her. However, the maid had discovered that John was really a woman and had informed the Reverend. On her leaving, the Reverend gave her a letter of reference and said,

'Here John, take this character — and now tell me seriously, are you a man or a woman?'

'A man', she replied, and left quickly.

Later she became a servant to Mr. Clarke, the landlord of the Navigation Inn at Shardlow. After some three months she was attacked and beaten, and therefore she left. While at Shardlow, Matilda Lacy met and fell in love with her, which was another reason for leaving. Unfortunately, Matilda was pregnant by a married man and it was therefore desirable to get married quickly. Both Matilda and her mother followed John. Eventually she had to reveal to them that she was a woman and so what they proposed was impossible. John moved from job to job, but was so continually hounded by these two that in the end she consented to the marriage. They were married in Aston Church by the Reverend Murphy. For three years John supported Matilda and her child by working in Derby as a bricklayer's labourer. Finally she could stand this state of affairs no longer and told her landlady, Mrs. Dawson, the whole story. Mrs. Dawson wasted no time in dealing with the Lacys and gave Harriet women's clothes to wear, as well as money to keep herself now that she could not work as before. Harriet was at this time twenty years old, and in 1826 when all this was revealed it caused quite a sensation in Derby. A small book was published, titled, A SHORT SKETCH OF THE LIFE AND ADVENTURES OF HARRIET BRIDGET MOORE, OTHERWISE JOHN MURPHY. A ballad was also written. Not long afterwards she married a Mr. Gardiner.

Sophia Locke, alias John Smith:

Sophia was born in a cave near Crober Wood in Sutton in about 1788. Since the rest of the family were boys, she wore men's clothes from the age of 3 onwards. She lived in Glossop, New Mills, was married in Winster Church and eventually died in Macclesfield in 1848. It was not until her death that her secret was revealed to the public. The Macclesfield Courier had the headline, 'Singular case of concealment of sex'.

On Saturday, September 16, 1848, Mr. Bland, one of the medical officers of the Macclesfield Union, was asked to see John Smith, who was suffering from dysentery. Her voice and facial features were so like a woman's that Mr. Bland was suspicious. He questioned Mrs. McCann, the landlady of the house, and she replied,

'I don't know, Doctor; all I can tell you is that he
and his wife have lodged here nine weeks, and he has
always dressed as a man, and followed his occupation
as knife grinder and spoon maker.'

Mr. Bland saw John's wife, and she informed him that though they were not married they were living together and that she had eleven children. For the moment Mr. Bland was content, but subsequent visits to his patient aroused his suspicions. A week later Sophia died, and Mr. Bland was able to certify instantly that she was a woman. His wife sewed the body up in a sheet so that no-one else would know. As to the eleven children, she had had these from a former marriage.

Shortly afterwards the rest of Sophia's story became known. Near where she was born she was known as a woman following a fight, which she won. Her shirt was ripped open exposing her upper body. In about 1823 she was in Winster. Here a gentleman offered her £5 to marry a servant of his who had become pregnant. They were married soon afterwards in Winster Church. The servant gave birth to a daughter, and all three lived together for some seven years. She lived with other women after that, until she met her last 'wife' in New Mills, fourteen years before her death. Sophia promised her that she would maintain the family, a promise she kept.

THE WOMAN WHO ATE PINS

Kitty Hudson, who is often named the human pincushion, was born in Arnold in Nottinghamshire in 1765. When she was six years old she moved to Nottingham and lived with her grandfather, who was the sexton of St. Mary's Church there. Her grandfather, Mr. White, employed a maid-servant who regularly swept the church. Kitty always accompanied her when doing this task, for she would be given some toffee for every mouthful of pins she accumulated. As time passed this pin-collecting became a natural habit, and she found that she could not sleep or eat without pins in her mouth. Often in the middle of the night she would slip out of bed for a mouthful of pins before being able to fall asleep. This practice was naturally ruining her health. Her double teeth were worn down and she complained of numbness in her limbs and of lack of sleep. At length she was taken to hospital.

At the hospital she underwent a series of operations, during which time pins, needles and pieces of bone were removed from all over her body. On June 12, 1785, she was discharged as finally cured. A man named John Goddard, who from childhood days had been in love with Kitty, happened to be at the hospital at the same time as Kitty, having an eye removed. His devotion to Kitty helped her through her ordeal, and he told her that he would marry her even if she lost all her limbs. Six months after she left the hospital she married John. He was a man-servant to a gentleman who lived at Arnold. By him she had nineteen children, none of whom lived over the age of eighteen.

Following the death of John Goddard, Kitty went to live in Pinxton village in Derbyshire. Not long afterwards she remarried, to Henry Ludlam of South Wingfield, where she lived until she died aged seventy. One of Ludlam's sons, by his first marriage, confirmed that the following is correct.

'Kitty is said to have been of tall stature, nearly six feet in height, and although she had been dismissed as cured, the pins and needles still kept appearing at intervals until her death. A black spot would appear and then fester, and the pin's head would appear, which was drawn out. These came out in all parts of her body. Her general health was good and she pursued her ordinary avocations without personal inconvenience, except from old age.'

I have come across another lady who ate pins. In November 1779, Mary Spelmore, who lived in St. Peter's Parish, Derby, was busy hanging out her washing. In her mouth she held the pins, and a sudden swaying of the lines caused her to swallow a mouthful. She became violently ill and was taken to the hospital in Nottingham. Both her left side and shoulder swelled up and, after bursting, numerous pins came out. After five months at the hospital she was released and pronounced cured.

HALTER DEVIL CHAPEL

In the small village of Muggington, two miles north west of Kedleston, in South Derbyshire, is reputedly the smallest episcopal church in England. It is known as Halter Devil Chapel, and forms part of a farmhouse. This is the tale as to how it came to be built. In the early eighteenth century, Francis Brown was an avid drinker and was frequently drunk. One night he became so drunk that he told his wife he would ride to Derby on his horse. He added, boastfully, that he would do so even if he had to 'halter the Devil'. He staggered out, and finding his saddle he went to put it onto his horse. Feeling around he was astonished to find that his horse had horns. He dropped the saddle and passed out. When he recovered, he vowed to give up his drinking and build a chapel; both of which he did. He had in fact mistaken a cow for his horse. The chapel was built in 1723 and originally had the following inscription -

> 'Francis Brown, in his old age,
> Did build him here an hermitage.'

to which later was added -

> 'Who being old and full of evil,
> Once on a time haltered the Devil.'

DOVERIDGE YEW TREE

Many of the churchyards of Derbyshire have very old and venerable yew trees, such as the one at Churchtown near Matlock, which is believed to be 1,800 years old. The yew tree at Doveridge, in the south-western corner of the county, is not as old as that, but is estimated to be 1,400 years old, and thus the second oldest in the county. When the tree was last measured, the trunk, which is now hollow, was found to be 22 feet in circumference, and the outermost branches were found to encircle an area with a perimeter of 260 feet. According to a tradition, under the yawning branches of the tree Robin Hood and Maid Marion were married.

SWARKESTONE BRIDGE

SWARKESTON BRIDGE

'Swarkeston, when I behold that pleasant sight
Whose river runs a progress with delight,
Joyed with the beauties of fresh flowery plaines
And bounteous fields that crown the Plow-man's pains.'

By Thomas Bancroft, who was born at
Swarkeston, and taken from his
collection of EPIGRAMS, published in 1639.

Swarkeston Bridge lies some five miles south of Derby and is remarkable for being three quarters of a mile long. There is a somewhat sad tale of its origin. Tradition states that the bridge was built in the thirteenth century by two sisters. Part of the present bridge, which is largely seventeenth and eighteenth century, dates from this period. These two sisters had just become engaged and were celebrating the event with their fiances. Part way through the celebrations the men were called away to a meeting on the other side of the river Trent. While they were away a torrential storm blew up which swelled the river and flooded the plain, which is the reason why the bridge is so long. The two fiances returned, but were drowned in their attempt to cross the turbulent flooded river. The two sisters erected the bridge in their memory and maintained it for the rest of their unmarried lives.

MELBOURNE POOL

On the south side of Melbourne Hall, at the southern tip of Derbyshire, is a large pool known as Melbourne Pool. It is said that the water covers the quarry from which the stone was extracted to build Melbourne Castle. The castle was built about the beginning of the fourteenth century, but by 1460 it was a ruined shell. Today only one wall is left to the rear of the buildings of Castle Farm, a quarter of a mile north from the pool. The castle served as a prison for the Duke of Bourbon, who was captured at the Battle of Agincourt on October 25, 1415. The governor of the castle was Sir Ralph Shirley, who was one of the commanders of the battle, and three miles south of there in Staunton Herald Church can be seen the banner which he captured. The Duke of Bourbon was held prisoner at the castle for nineteen years before being released for a ransom of £18,000. He died before he could leave England.

MELBOURNE POOL

HANGMAN'S STONE

Hangman's Stone lies approximately one mile north west of the village of Ticknall, in south Derbyshire, at Grid Reference SK342252. Originally it was upright, but it now lies horizontally. According to the legend, a sheep stealer was on his way home with his catch, carrying the sheep on his back secured by a rope. When he reached the upright stone, he decided to have a rest and placed the sheep on the top while he leant against the stone. Without warning the sheep slipped and fell down one side, and the rope went across his throat and strangled the stealer.

> 'The burden had slipp'd, and his neck it had nipp'd:
> He was hanged by his prize — all was clear.'

THE DEATH OF A TREE

Coton-in-the-Elms, at the southern tip of Derbyshire, has a sad tale regarding one of its trees. On March 31, 1644, a soldier, Phillip Greensmith, who deserted his regiment, was executed on a tree there. In silent sympathy with the dead man, the tree slowly died as well.

SUPERSTITIONS AND SAYINGS OF DERBYSHIRE

DERBYSHIRE FOLK RHYMES

1. 'Though valley sheep are fatter,
The Highland sheep are sweeter.'

2. Epitaph from a gravestone in Taddington Church -
'Farewell to you our children dear,
We've toiled for you for many a year;
We've always tried to do our best.
And now we've gone to take our rest.'

3. 'When Codnor's pond runs dry
The Lords may say good-bye.'

4. 'Derbyshire born, Derbyshire bred,
Strong i' th'arm, and thick i' th' yed.' (head)

5. 'Baslow for Gentlefolks,
Calver for trenchers,
Middleton for rogues and thieves,
And Eyam for pretty wenches.'

6. 'The cuckoo is a merry bird,
She sings as she flies;
She brings us good tidings,
And tells us no lies.
She sucks little birds' eggs,
To make her voice clear,
That she may sing Cuckoo
Three months in the year.'

7. 'Ashford in the Water,
Bakewell in the Spice,
Sheldon in the Nutwood,
Longstone in the Lice.'

8. 'Cheshire for men. Barkshire for Dogges;
Bedfordshire for naked flesh;
And Lincolnshire for Bogges,
Derbyshire for lead; Devonshire for Tinne;
Wiltshire for Hunting Plaines;
And Middlesex for Sinne.'

9. 'Winster Wakes, there's ale and cakes,
Elton Wakes, there's trenchers;
Bircher Wakes, there's knives and forks,
Wensley Wakes, there's wenches.'

10. 'Pinder pipers,
Bradda rappers,
Smawder smokers
Come to lick Castleton swill tubs.'
(Pinder means Pindale; Bradda — Bradwell;
Smawder — Smalldale; and Rappers -
rascal thieves.)

11. The following is a Bretton rhyme, dated about 1860.
'Matthey Elliott lives at 'fowd (fold),
An' that, ah think, is varry cow'd,
Mr. Moorhouse lives at'side,
An' Dinah Cooper's full o' pride.'
Deciphered, this means that Elliott lived at Ivy House, John Moorhouse at Nether Bretton
Farm, and Dinah Cooper lived in a cottage beside the farm.

STONE FOLKLORE

1. Close to Baslow Edge is the Eagle Stone. The name eagle is derived from the God, Aigle,
who is reputed to be able to
lift boulders no man can lift. It is also said that when a
cock crows the stone turns round! The stone is also known
as a lover's stone; for in the olden days, before a couple
could get married, the man had to prove himself by scaling
the rock.

EAGLE STONE

2. In Faybrick Wood at Ashover is a wishing stone. By sitting
on the stone and wishing three times your wish will come true. In the Ashover district are two other stones of
interest — the Cuckoo Stone and the Cock-Crowing Stone.

3. Two miles south east of Wirksworth is Alport Height, which
is owned by the National Trust. On a clear day the view
from the summit, 1,034 feet, extends to six counties.
Just below the summit is the twenty foot high Alport Stone.
This, like the Eagle Stone, is a lover's stone, and custom
was that the man had to climb to the top of this before he
could get married.

4. At the northern end of Matlock, overlooking Lumsdale, is a
wishing stone. It is situated about a quarter of a mile
left of the Chesterfield road, at Grid Reference SK308606.
The stone is reached by walking along Asker Lane beside
the Duke of Wellington Inn. To gain your wish, you must
sit on the stone and wish — your dream will come true.

MATLOCK'S WISHING STONE

SOME DERBYSHIRE SAYINGS, although many are universally known.

1. 'Save yore breath to cool yore porridge.' — said by person who remains indifferent to scolding.

2. 'Thar't loik a chip i porridge.' — said about a person who is low in intelligence.

3. 'Thou'd mak a beggar beat his bag.' — a retort to an obstinate or stubborn person.

4. 'That's a foolish bird as fouls its own nest.' — said to a careless person.

5. 'Docks grow beside o'nettles.' — meaning that troubles are always accompanied by mercies and blessings.

6. 'Thagh knows noi lad, a black hen leys whoit eggs.' - self-evident.

7. 'Oi'll giet thee, afore th' cat's licked her ear.' - a promise made in anger which will never be carried out.

8. 'Teach thy Granny t' suck eggs.' — said by person to another who is trying to convince them of something untrue or improbable.

9. 'Oi'll dowt by hook or by crook.' — determined to do it.

10. 'It's no use crying o'er shed milk.' — said by person to another who is worrying over something which has happened and he cannot now change.

11. 'Care will kill a cat.' — meaning do not be over-cautious.

12. 'Sue a beggar and catch a louse.' — said as a warning to those who think of reporting an incident to the Police.

13. 'He shot a pigeon and kilt a crow.' — said about someone who hit another target than the one he had aimed for.

14. 'Loil an onion, aw peelin.' — said about someone who is wearing too many clothes.

SOME DERBYSHIRE SUPERSTITIONS

1. If a fire throws out a piece of coal, wood or stone, it should be carefully inspected. If it is in the shape of a coffin, the person finding it will die soon.

2. If pieces of burning coal attach themselves to a fire grate, separate them by blowing. The number of blows needed is the number of days before strangers call on a visit.

3. If a cat sits before a fire a lot, a storm can be expected. A black cat is very lucky for its owner, but it must be totally black with no white hairs. If your cat sits at the window purring and looks out, good luck can be expected.

4. If you see a bright spark from a candle, you can expect a letter. If the spark falls off, you can expect the letter the following day.

5. If you twirl a chair in front of the owner, bad luck will befall you.

6. If tea leaves float on top of your cup, a stranger will call. To discover when, place the leaves on the back of your hand. The number of blows needed to remove them equals the number of days before your visitor will arrive.

7. At New Year, a visit from a dark man is considered very lucky.

8. You should never pass anybody on the stairs; to do so will bring you bad luck.

9. To dream of lice is a sign of death.

To dream of pulling out teeth is a sign of bad luck.

To dream of finding a large sum of money is a sign that you will lose money.

10. If you are ill in bed and a bird flies straight into the window, you know that death is at hand.

11. You should never move your belongings to your new home on a Friday. To do so will bring you bad luck.

12. You should never look through the window at a new moon. It is unlucky if you do. When you do look at a new moon, turn over whatever money you have in your pocket, for luck.

13. If you see a black snail, pick it up and throw it over
your left shoulder. This will bring you good luck.

14. If you hear either whistling maidens or crowing hens, it
is a sign of bad luck.

15. If a new born lamb comes out head first, all will be well.
If it comes out tail first, the farmer can expect a year
of bad luck.

16. If you meet a funeral procession at twilight from the
opposite direction, you must observe the coffin. If no
lights can be seen from it, you know all is well. If
you see lights, it is an advance warning that your death
is nigh.

17. If you see one or more magpies flying in the air -
One for a wedding,
Two for a birth,
Three for sorrow,
And four for mirth.

It depends on where you live in Derbyshire (and what you
want to believe!) for this is another version -
One for a death,
Two for mirth,
Three for a wedding,
Four for a birth.

18. When you hear a cuckoo for the first time each year -
If you have gold in your pocket,
you will have plenty all year.
If you have silver in your pocket,
you will always have enough for the year.
If you have copper in your pocket,
you will never be without any.
Should you hear the bird on your right,
it is a sign of good luck.
But hear it on your left and it is a
sign of bad luck.

19. A white spot on the finger or nail is a sign of a gift
coming:

'A gift on the thumb
Is sure to come:
A gift on the finger
Is sure to linger.'

20. After having your hair cut, throw the cut hair on the
fire. If it blazes well, you know all is alright.
If it does not blaze, you can expect an illness.

21. Peacock feathers brought into the house are a sign of an illness or even death to the occupiers.

22. Farmers' weather lore -
a) If hens gather on high ground, rain is coming.
b) If the cock stays on the roost longer than usual and crows, you can expect a wet spell.
c) If tame geese suddenly fly, it is a sign of approaching bad weather.
d) If cattle graze at the highest point of a field, a storm is approaching.

23. The person who kills either a wren or robin will be unlucky in the future.

24. A green or mild winter makes a fat churchyard.

25. If hips and haws are plentiful in autumn, it is a sign of a hard, frosty winter; because Providence has taken care to provide for the birds.

26. If a person goes on a message and turns back before it is accomplished, it is unlucky for all concerned.

27. If you hear a cock crowing at night, it is a sign that either death or illness is at hand.

28. If you hear a dog howling at night, this is also indicative of some sad happening.

29. If you lay a walking stick upon the table, it will bring you bad luck.

30. When laying a table and two knives cross, it is a sign that you will quarrel in the immediate future.

31. If two people speak together on the same subject at the same time, or speak the same word simultaneously, they should make a wish, and the wish will be granted providing they do not divulge what they have wished for.

32. Derbyshire people once believed that there was a world before this one, and that there will be a world after this one. After that, it is the end.

33. Derbyshire people at one time preferred to take the oath on salt instead of the Bible.

34. In days gone by, when a cow died, Derbyshire people used to bury the animal beneath a fruitful tree in the orchard.

35. If you see a ghost, walk round it nine times and it will disappear.

36. If a ghost appears before you, say to it, 'In the name of the Lord, why visited thou me?' The ghost will answer and inform you why he has come.

37. If an old woman comes begging to your door, never give her any silver. If you do, she will have power over you.

38. To keep a witch out of your house, place a horseshoe with the 'U' shape driven into the ground, outside near the front door.

39. Another way to keep a witch out of your premises is to plant a Mountain Ash tree in your garden. This tree is known as the 'Witch-Wiggin' tree.

DERBYSHIRE SUPERSTITIONS REGARDING DEATH AND BURIAL.

1. When you have a corpse in the house and bake some bread, the dough will not rise.

2. If you have a corpse in the house and go out, do not lock all the doors and windows. Leave a window open at least, so that the spirit can fly away.

3. Derbyshire people are said to be buried with their feet pointing east, towards the Mount of Olives, upon which Christ will appear on the Day of Resurrection.

4. Funeral wine is first given to the corpse bearers. The guests do not have any until after the completion of the burial.

5. True to many Derbyshire legends — a dying man who has 'something on his mind' cannot die until he has revealed what troubles him.

6. An invalid's teeth are kept in a jar until he dies, when they are placed in the coffin. It is said that you must account for your teeth when you reach Heaven. People at the funeral may say, 'Have you got his teeth in the coffin?' or, 'Don't bury him without his teeth.'.

7. In Dore, which was once part of Derbyshire, the corpse was laid out in the house. A pewter plate containing salt was placed upon the chest so that no witch would interfere with the deceased.

8. The first person to meet a funeral will be the next to die. It is recorded that a woman from Dronfield always followed a funeral so that she would see who was next to go.

9. Corpses laid out in houses in Eckington were always placed near some food.

10. In North Derbyshire the burial procession for an unmarried girl was one of tradition. Eight girls dressed in white, who were her friends, would carry the deceased to church. Their route had to follow a main road and never a minor one. If they came to a chapel or church where the deceased used to visit, they had to stop and sing a hymn.

SUPERSTITIONS OF THE COUNTRYSIDE

1. If a man cuts down a young ash tree, the man can be expected to be banned from the parish. The ash tree is known as the 'Tree of the Peak'.

2. Derbyshire people will not burn any elder wood on their fire. They believe that Christ was crucified on a cross made from elder wood.

3. When you go bilberry or blackberry picking each year, you must throw the first one over your head and say, 'Pray God send me good luck today.'.

4. If you have a strong fear of snakes, place a raw onion beside you and no snake will come anywhere near you.

5. In the early summer when the bees begin to be a nuisance, kill the first one that enters your house. You will be troubled no more by them for the rest of the year.

SOME DERBYSHIRE CURES

1. If you are stung by nettles, rub a dock leaf on the
affected area and say repeatedly:-
'Nettle come out
and dock go in.'

2. If you happen to burn or scald yourself, place on the
affected area a plaster of fresh cow-dung.

3. If you suffer from warts upon your hand, go to a marsh and
collect some rushes. Tie a knot in each rush until you
have the same number of rushes as warts. Touch each wart
with a separate rush knot before burying them in the
ground. As the rushes decompose in the ground, so will
the warts slowly disappear from your hand.

4. At Brandside, near Dove Head and some four miles south of
Buxton, was found in 1890 the following written charm for
the cure of toothache. It should be repeated several
times to have any effect:-

'Peter stood at the gate of Jerusalem weeping,
and the Lord said unto Peter, "Why weepest thou,
Peter?" And he said, "Lord, I am sore troubled
with the toothache. Grant, Lord, that he (or
she) that is troubled thou may help them in the
name of the Father and of the Son and of the Holy
Ghost. Amen."

5. If you suffer from any form of skin disease, soak some
gunpowder in hot water and compress it into a pulp.
Then spread the paste over the affected area.

6. If you have a nose bleed, take the key out of the most
outer door of your house and put it onto the back of your
neck.

7. If you suffer from consumption, dig a hole in the ground
large enough for your head. Lie face down on the ground
with your head in the hole. Lie here for half an hour
breathing into the hole. The treatment should be carried
out each morning until you are cured.

DERBYSHIRE FAIRIES

1. Derbyshire fairies are said to be 'little beings about a yard high which are always jumping up and down'. Derbyshire dwarfs, on the other hand, are 'very small, pretty-featured people, who run about in the chinks and fissures of rocks'.

2. Derbyshire women used to make their yeast for oatcakes the night before and leave it on the kitchen table for the 'little people'. In the night they could be heard mixing it.

3. A field at Calver, known as Stocking Field, was a popular place for watching the dancing fairies. Here at dusk they would dance in a circle with a female fairy in the middle. She was known as the midwife and was always blindfolded.

4. When a woman is about to give birth, fairies will always come and leave only when the child is born.

5. In Eckington the women always used to sweep the hearth every night before going to bed. If asked why they did this, they would reply that if they did not the fairies would not come and bring them presents.

6. At Moorwood Hall Farm, near Holmesfield, the woman of the house locked the house up to attend her daughter's funeral. On her return the house although completely empty was clean and tidy and a fire burned in the grate. It is said that this was the work of the fairies.

7. The people of Curbar used to say that Morris dancing, which still takes place in Tideswell and Winster in the summer, was really fairy dancing.

8. If any woman of Curbar made cream, she always took a bowl of it up onto Curbar Edge for the fairies. Although no-one ever saw any, the bowl was always empty when they returned to fetch it.

9. Miners in north Derbyshire used to leave a hundredweight bag of coal in the pit, every week, for the fairies.

10. On Easter Sunday in Bradwell the children used to drop pins down the five wells of the village. They said that a fairy lived at each well and knew whether a child had dropped in a pin or not. On Easter Monday the children would walk around with bottles containing sweetmeat. The bottles of the children who had not dropped pins into the wells broke, whilst the bottles of the ones who had dropped pins remained intact.

DERBYSHIRE GHOSTS

1. A tale is told that a mother was so upset at her daughter's death that she did not sleep for eleven weeks. At this time her daughter appeared and said to her, 'Mother, if you grieve for me thus I cannot rest in the Kingdom of Heaven.' Her mother went to bed and slept.

2. A baker and his wife who lived in a secluded house in Stoney Middleton were frequently visited by the ghost of a murdered woman who had previously lived there. Every time she came she made holes in the newly-baked bread. One night the baker and his wife waited for her to come, but never saw her although the holes still appeared in the bread.

3. At Highlow Hall, a former residence of the Eyre family, it is said that at midnight a man dressed in white and riding a white horse can be seen riding in the immediate vicinity.

4. On the common at Coal Aston were seen three spectres. The first was three thin women standing in a line, each holding an hour glass. The second was a giant some nine feet high, carrying an oak tree over his shoulder. The third was a normal-sized man carrying a scythe. The meaning of this is believed to be that the three-women spectre was a sign that the beholder had only three hours to live. The giant had come to inform him whether he was young or old, and the man with the scythe had come to cut him down.

5. To exorcise a spirit, repeat the following:-

'Jesus a name high over all
O'er earth, and air, and sea,
Before thy name the angels fall,
And devils fear and flee.'

WITCHCRAFT IN DERBYSHIRE

1. A favourite meeting place for witches to cast a spell on people was a cross-roads or 'four lane ends'.

2. Derbyshire women in the olden days always carried a cross made from 'witch-wiggin', or mountain ash. It was concealed under the dress and worn as protection against witchcraft.

3. A young girl was engaged to a man with light hair. The girl met a witch on her travels who told her she must marry a dark haired man. The witch gave the girl a triangular-shaped piece of paper which she pricked three times. The girl was to wear the paper next to her bosom, and three weeks later the paper would have the name of her dark-haired husband-to-be.

4. Living in Eckington was a woman who was reputed to be a witch. She always stayed in bed until noon. She was said to converse with the Devil, to whom she had sold herself, and to impose tough commands to people to do her will. On one occasion she commanded that a man go to bed so that she could have peace and quiet. He obeyed.

5. In Eyam lived a woman whom many regarded as being a witch. Before she bewitched anyone she rattled a canister full of 'horse nail stumps' in front of them.

6. Living in Holmesfield was an old woman known as a witch. She wore 'one of those hoods called little red riding hoods'.

7. At Killamarsh, near Chesterfield, lived a 'Wise Woman'. Whatever the difficulty, people came to her for help and advice. She was particularly adept at locating missing husbands, and is said never to have failed in this pursuit.

8. Near Dove Head and close to Axe Edge in North Derbyshire lived a witch. She charged a fee to all her visitors, and with this money she supported her idle son.

9. At the small hamlet of Crowdicote in the Upper Dove Valley lived the Crowdicote witch. A woman was about to leave after a consultation, and was told that she would meet a dark man on her way home. This man, whom she had never met before, would become her husband. The prediction came true.

OTHER BOOKS BY JOHN N. MERRILL PUBLISHED BY JNM PUBLICATIONS

DAY WALK GUIDES -

SHORT CIRCULAR WALKS IN THE PEAK DISTRICT
LONG CIRCULAR WALKS IN THE PEAK DISTRICT
CIRCULAR WALKS IN WESTERN PEAKLAND
SHORT CIRCULAR WALKS IN THE STAFFORDSHIRE MOORLANDS
PEAK DISTRICT TOWN WALKS
SHORT CIRCULAR WALKS AROUND MATLOCK
SHORT CIRCULAR WALKS IN THE DUKERIES
SHORT CIRCULAR WALKS IN SOUTH YORKSHIRE
SHORT CIRCULAR WALKS AROUND DERBY
SHORT CIRCULAR WALKS AROUND BUXTON
SHORT CIRCULAR WALKS AROUND NOTTINGHAMSHIRE
SHORT CIRCULAR WALKS ON THE NORTHERN MOORS
40 SHORT CIRCULAR PEAK DISTRICT WALKS
SHORT CIRCULAR WALKS IN THE HOPE VALLEY

INSTRUCTION & RECORD —

HIKE TO BE FIT . . . STROLLING WITH JOHN
THE JOHN MERRILL WALK RECORD BOOK

CANAL WALK GUIDES —

VOL ONE — DERBYSHIRE AND NOTTINGHAMSHIRE
VOL TWO — CHESHIRE AND STAFFORDSHIRE
VOL THREE — STAFFORDSHIRE
VOL FOUR — THE CHESHIRE RING

DAY CHALLENGE WALKS –

JOHN MERRILL'S PEAK DISTRICT CHALLENGE WALK
JOHN MERRILL'S YORKSHIRE DALES CHALLENGE WALK
JOHN MERRILL'S NORTH YORKSHIRE MOORS CHALLENGE WALK
PEAK DISTRICT END TO END WALKS
THE LITTLE JOHN CHALLENGE WALK
JOHN MERRILL'S LAKELAND CHALLENGE WALK
JOHN MERRILL'S STAFFORDSHIRE MOORLAND CHALLENGE WALK
JOHN MERRILL'S DARK PEAK CHALLENGE WALK

MULTIPLE DAY WALKS —

THE RIVERS' WAY
PEAK DISTRICT HIGH LEVEL ROUTE
PEAK DISTRICT MARATHONS
THE LIMEY WAY
THE PEAKLAND WAY

COAST WALKS —

ISLE OF WIGHT COAST WALK
PEMBROKESHIRE COAST PATH
THE CLEVELAND WAY

HISTORICAL GUIDES —

DERBYSHIRE INNS
HALLS AND CASTLES OF THE PEAK DISTRICT & DERBYSHIRE
TOURING THE PEAK DISTRICT AND DERBYSHIRE BY CAR
DERBYSHIRE FOLKLORE
LOST INDUSTRIES OF DERBYSHIRE
PUNISHMENT IN DERBYSHIRE
CUSTOMS OF THE PEAK DISTRICT AND DERBYSHIRE
WINSTER — A VISITOR'S GUIDE
ARKWRIGHT OF CROMFORD
TALES FROM THE MINES by GEOFFREY CARR

JOHN'S MARATHON WALKS —

TURN RIGHT AT LAND'S END
WITH MUSTARD ON MY BACK
TURN RIGHT AT DEATH VALLEY
EMERALD COAST WALK

COLOUR GUIDES —

THE PEAK DISTRICT . . . Something to remember her by.

SKETCH BOOKS — by John Creber

NORTH STAFFORDSHIRE SKETCHBOOK